OLYMPIC
★
TITANIC
★
BRITANNIC

Olympic cut an impressive profile when she left Belfast for her sea
trials on 28 May 1911. (Günter Bäbler collection)

OLYMPIC

★

TITANIC

★

BRITANNIC

AN ILLUSTRATED HISTORY OF
THE 'OLYMPIC' CLASS SHIPS

MARK CHIRNSIDE

'As she lay abreast the stage yesterday the general opinion among the many thousands of sightseers who thronged both banks of the river was that the Mersey had never borne a ship of more beautiful proportions or more graceful lines. So exceedingly well balanced are the proportions of the vessel that at first glance her vast bulk is hardly realised; indeed it is impossible for the eye to form any complete vision of the tremendous size of the vessel without comparison; that is until some other vessel becomes dwarfed by her vicinity…'

The Journal of Commerce describes Olympic's visit to Liverpool, 2 June 1911.

Britannic, serving as a hospital ship, leaves Naples for Southampton on the afternoon of 4 February 1916. (Mark Chirnside/Michail Michailakis collection)

First published 2012

The History Press
The Mill, Brimscombe Port
Stroud, Gloucestershire, GL5 2QG
www.thehistorypress.co.uk

© Mark Chirnside, 2012

The right of Mark Chirnside to be identified as the Author of this work has been asserted in accordance with the Copyrights, Designs and Patents Act 1988.

British Library Cataloguing in Publication Data.
A catalogue record for this book is available from the British Library.

ISBN 978 0 7524 5310 1

Typesetting and origination by The History Press
Printed in India
Manufacturing managed by Jellyfish Print Solutions Ltd

Front cover: Olympic's towering hull, then the largest moving man-made object on earth, is in its natural element after launch on the morning of 20 October 1910. (Topical Press Agency/Getty Images)

Back Cover: Passengers line the decks as Olympic enters New York for the first time on the morning of 21 June 1911. It was perhaps the proudest moment in Captain Smith's career. (Library of Congress, Prints and Photographs Division)

CONTENTS

INTRODUCTION

This volume is intended to provide a concise illustrated history of the 'Olympic' class ships. For those new to the subject, it should serve as a useful introduction and a good general overview of the three ships. Those with a long-standing interest in the topic may be sceptical that there is any further new or original information to be learned, but that scepticism will prove unfounded. The images selected are not an exhaustive look at each and every aspect of each vessel's life, but as a whole they cover a wide variety of subjects related to all three ships. What might be lacking in quantity is made up for in originality; a considerable number of them are rare or have never been seen in print before.

Several myths have been dispelled, but the focus is more on the human stories: the experiences and feelings of the people who planned and built the ships, and of those who went to sea in them. Although *Titanic* and the disaster that befell her are an integral part of the 'Olympic' class ships' history, the details of the disaster have purposely been avoided. It is far beyond the scope of this volume, and the subject has been covered adequately in a large number of works dedicated to that specific subject. The lesser-known *Britannic* features at *Titanic*'s expense.

This book can be considered a companion to the comprehensive single-volume history, *The 'Olympic' Class Ships: Olympic, Titanic & Britannic*, which was published as a revised and expanded edition in May 2011.

Mark Chirnside
February 2012

LEGEND AND REALITY

A PROGRESSIVE SCIENCE

The 'Olympic' class liners came from a long line of successful ships produced by the White Star Line's enduring association with the venerable Belfast shipbuilding firm of Harland & Wolff. Given the fierce competition at the turn of the twentieth century, the Anglo-German naval race was mirrored by the struggle for supremacy between individual shipping lines.

White Star's ownership was complex. It was registered in Britain as the Oceanic Steam Navigation Company, but it traded as the White Star Line. J. Bruce Ismay, son of the line's late founder, was chairman and managing director; William James Pirrie, of Harland & Wolff, who was made a peer in 1906, and Harold Sanderson completed the directors. The American banker J.P. Morgan set his sights on the line and acquired a controlling interest in it through his firm J.P. Morgan & Co. in 1902. His intention was to form an enormous combine with interests in the major shipping lines. Thereafter, almost all the line's shares were held by the International Navigation Company, registered in Liverpool; in turn, that company's shares were held by the International Mercantile Marine Company (IMM), an American entity based in New Jersey and controlled by J.P. Morgan & Co. In 1904, Morgan appointed J. Bruce Ismay as IMM's president to whip the combine into shape.[1] He remained the White Star Line's chairman and managing director. By 1911, the various lines within IMM had 120 vessels with a gross tonnage of 1,067,425 tons, and there were six steamers accounting for 113,700 tons being built.

The White Star Line's own profits rose from £454,024 in 1901 to £1,073,752 in 1911, as they expanded a large and modern fleet. Focusing on comfort and luxury rather than speed, White Star could reap the benefits of lower operating costs. They were demonstrated by four large sister ships, known collectively as the 'Big Four': *Celtic*, *Cedric*, *Baltic* and *Adriatic*. When *Celtic* entered service in 1901, she was the largest liner in the world, but not the fastest. She had an enormous capacity for passengers and cargo. *Celtic*'s piston-based reciprocating engines drove two propellers and gave an economical service speed of 16 knots. She was a comfortable ship and generated substantial profits.

Adriatic completed the quartet, arriving in New York for the first time on 16 May 1907. She carried over 2,500 passengers and the *New York Times* reported:

> She is a stately and dignified craft, and among all the saloon passengers who crossed in her there was not one who did not agree with the officers that there is not a better vessel afloat when it comes to steadiness in rough seas, easy going in smooth ones, and general all around comfort in all kinds of weather. The liner is one of the most luxuriously appointed afloat, and is in a class by herself in that she is equipped with a modern Turkish Bath apartment, in addition to all the other innovations.

Adriatic had sailed from Liverpool, but her return saw her go to Southampton to complete the company's Southampton–Cherbourg–Queenstown–New

In March 1908, the *New York Times* compared the White Star Line's first *Oceanic* with *Lusitania* (1907) and the new '1,000ft' liners expected to enter service. Although the '*Olympic*' class ships were actually less than 900ft in overall length, they were still significantly larger. It is interesting that this early depiction shows *Olympic* with only three funnels. Journalist George Horne told a story some years later, after a German liner had taken *Olympic*'s place as the largest liner in the world. He explained that 'the dark flowering of smoke above the deck meant power, speed and comfort; the more stacks the more smoke and power. This belief, strongly held then among foreign-born travellers, was recognised by an old-time agent who had difficulty closing an excursion booking for some Americans bent on a visit to their native land'. Horne continued:

On the agent's walls were two large pictures, one showing the *Imperator* (later to become the *Berengaria*) with the Statue of Liberty in the background beyond the three stacks. The other picture showed the *Olympic* at sea… flaunting four

stacks. The leader of the excursion party, with two hundred round trip tickets at stake, gazed with admiration and surprise at the four stacks. He wanted everyone transferred to the *Olympic*. He would not accept the explanation that it was really a slightly smaller ship, although one of the Atlantic queens. Finally the crafty agent played his ace.

'I'll let you in on a secret,' he explained. 'The port of New York taxes ships according to the number of their stacks. Actually, my friend, the *Imperator* has five stacks, but just before coming into New York they lower two of them. They'll be put up again as soon as you pass the Statue of Liberty.' The traveller was delighted. Five stacks! And the deal was closed.

It may be apocryphal, but it is an interesting story. (Digital restoration by James Samwell, © 2011/*New York Times*)

York express service. Operating with the earlier White Star liners *Teutonic*, *Majestic* and *Oceanic*, from then on the company's main express service operated out of Southampton rather than Liverpool. The change of policy helped attract continental passengers who could board when the ships called at Cherbourg, rather than having to cross the Channel first. Meanwhile, *Adriatic's* older sisters operated on the Liverpool to New York route with the smaller *Arabic*.

It was in these circumstances that White Star's rival, the Cunard Line, introduced *Lusitania* and *Mauretania* later in 1907. Far larger than *Adriatic*, at over 31,000 gross tons each, both ships were propelled by turbine engines and proved exceptionally fast. Cunard's express service continued to operate from Liverpool, and their new liners were capable of maintaining an average speed of more than 25 knots. Cunard had been assisted by a low interest loan from the British government, eager to support the company and maintain the British firm outside IMM. Even if White Star did not want to set speed records, they needed to respond. *Teutonic* and *Majestic* were more than fifteen years old.

'QUEEN OF THE SEAS'

The answer was to build larger and more luxurious liners. Although J. Bruce Ismay and Lord Pirrie reportedly discussed plans for two new liners in the summer of 1907, with the potential for a third to follow,[2] they had known even earlier that they would need to respond to Cunard. *Lusitania* and *Mauretania* had taken several years to build and were launched in 1906. The orders for *Olympic* (Yard Number 400) and *Titanic* (Yard Number 401) were first recorded on 30 April 1907.[3]

Just as *Adriatic* had been an improvement on her older sisters, the new liners would mark a great stride forward compared to previous White Star liners. *Adriatic's* first-class accommodation featured the usual smoke room and lounge, complimented by a reading and writing room, on the boat deck level. Down below, the first-class dining saloon was spacious and a gymnasium and Turkish Bath establishment were available. Although described as the first swimming bath on board a liner, the pool was rather small for the purpose and called a 'plunge bath'. In addition to the first-class suites, even some first-class staterooms had private baths. At the time, private bathrooms were a considerable luxury.

Newspaper reports began to appear as early as the summer of 1907, although rumours often had little to do with the real facts and reports were contradictory. In August 1907, an American newspaper reported that 'two new steamers' were being built for the Southampton service; while *Lusitania* was in the midst of her maiden voyage to New York the following month, more information became public. As the *New York Times* put it: 'Bigger than the *Lusitania*: White Star Line Decides to Build Vessel – Speed to be 22 knots.' No reference was made to two ships, merely an admission that Harland & Wolff were 'working upon plans for a new White Star liner which is to be bigger than the *Lusitania*.' It was an interesting attempt to distract attention from the new Cunarder. An interesting interview was given by J. Bruce Ismay in March 1908. Although no names were included, the reporter made persistent reference to steamers 1,000ft long, which was a remarkable exaggeration. Certainly, Ismay was coy when it came to details. Asked about the two ships' features, he replied: 'I may not tell you that, for if I did all our competitors would know, but I will repeat what I just said that they will be far ahead of anything that has yet been projected.' The reporter calculated:

> That if the rate of increase in steamship dimensions should be maintained for the next hundred years at the same ratio that they increased from 1807 to 1907, the ship launched at the end of the next century would have a speed of 6,527 knots a day, and would be able to cross from New York to England in about thirteen hours. The vessel would be nearly a mile in length and would have accommodations for 33,000 passengers…

The liners' names do not appear to have been confirmed publicly until April 1908. *Olympic*'s name was announced in a reporter's dispatch from Liverpool on 16 April 1908, and a week later her sister's followed. Although the choice

On 18 November 1909, work was advancing on *Titanic* (left); and *Olympic*'s hull (right) was almost fully framed. The ships were constructed on two slipways that had recently been completed and occupied part of the shipyard previously taken up by three smaller slipways. The huge Arroll gantry was a remarkable feat of engineering, which was completed in time for their construction and continued in use for decades. (*The Engineer*, 1909/Author's collection)

The World's Greatest Gantry, in Harland & Wolff's North Shipyard, Belfast.

As *Olympic*'s launch approached, the progress of construction was evident. *Olympic* and *Titanic*'s names were recorded in front of each ship. *Olympic*'s very light grey – almost white – hull presented an impressive sight. 'The expectant public will soon begin to count the weeks that intervene before the stately hull of the first ship can be seen riding in the water,' wrote the *New York Times* a few months before her launch: 'With the advanced condition of the shell of the *Olympic*, the hydraulic riveting, which is a notable feature, is coming into prominence; the symmetrical appearance of the rivet heads catches the eye and gives the impression of exceptional strength.' (Author's collection)

of *Olympic* was a topical one in light of the Olympic Games being hosted in London that year, in fact it had been considered by the White Star Line almost a decade earlier for a proposed sister ship to *Oceanic*, so it seems unlikely that the choice was entirely down to the Olympics of 1908. (Cunard had considered using the name *Olympia* when they were deciding upon the names of *Lusitania* and *Mauretania*, so in that sense it was lucky that the name was still available. It reflected the difference between Cunard and White Star nomenclature: while Cunard ships' names traditionally ended in 'ia', White Star's ended in 'ic.')

One unidentified observer, apparently from Harland & Wolff, made a number of notes about *Lusitania*, focusing on the smallest of details influencing passenger comfort: 'In some of the staterooms which are panelled with hard woods, there is a lot of creaking and noise when she is steaming into a head sea, and I should think that this is attributable entirely to the binding of the woodwork, as I remember quite well we had the same trouble in the *Majestic*

and the *Teutonic* years ago, and only overcame it by putting rubber strips between the panels of the woodwork'; 'I do not think any smoking should be allowed on this particular deck [B] forward of the expansion joint. To my knowledge, on several occasions ladies have had to leave their seats because men have been smoking pipes to windward of them, blowing ashes and smoke in their faces. There is any amount of smoking accommodation on the ship, and it seems to me most unnecessary that ladies who are not feeling particularly well should be bothered by inconsiderate men on practically the only bit of sheltered deck they have'; the lavatory door springs were 'quite useless when the ship is rolling' and hooks would be preferable: 'the best I have seen are those used in the White Star Line which automatically catch the door when pushed back, and merely require lifting to release…'; it would have been an improvement to have additional bathrooms amidships, as some first-class passengers had to make a long journey, while bathroom stewards were not always in attendance.

By 29 July 1908, J. Bruce Ismay and Harold Sanderson were able to visit Belfast with a party from the White Star Line to examine the shipbuilder's design work. They were greeted with an impressive sight: general arrangement plans for 'Design "D"' showed a long, elegant vessel with four funnels and a foremast. It envisaged accommodation for 600 first-class passengers, 716 second class and no fewer than 1,788 third class. Even though speed was not the first priority, the propelling machinery needed to be extremely powerful due to the vessel's size: the engine and boiler rooms took up more than two-thirds of the length of the ship. The outline showed an improved version of many of *Adriatic*'s features, with a remarkable amount of deck space for first-class passengers in particular. Unlike the earlier ship, where the bridge and officers' quarters were in separate deckhouses ahead of the main superstructure, *Olympic*'s bridge would be situated at the forward end of the boat deck. Fourteen main lifeboats and two smaller cutters were provided. It is easy to imagine them examining the plans, asking questions and making suggestions, but they clearly approved of the basic outline. The letter of agreement was signed for construction to proceed two days later. Following that agreement, attention turned to financing the project. Contrary to popular belief, J.P. Morgan did not bankroll it. The White Star Line mortgaged its existing fleet as security for its plan to issue bonds to the tune of £2,500,000, which would pay interest of 4.5 per cent. The first series of £1,250,000 were offered for public subscription in October 1908 and, from the proceeds, the company was able to meet the payments on the accounts of *Olympic* and *Titanic* as they fell due.[4]

As the plans were developed further, the design looked even better. *Adriatic*'s first-class passengers only had the use of a single lift (or 'elevator'),

Olympic's upper decks, seen in a rare photograph taken within weeks of her launch. Work is continuing on the deckhouses of the boat deck. At the forward end of the deck, a gap is visible at the middle of the steel bulwark, where the bridge will be constructed. Underneath, the deckhouses at the fore end of A-deck and B-deck would be fully painted by launch day.

To the bottom left of the picture, the four donkey boilers in the forward well deck provided a temporary steam supply to the ship's warping and anchor handling machinery. Temporary stairs are rigged for workmen's access, including one leading from the well deck to the forward end of B-deck (at the extreme left) and another two leading down the No.3 hatchway. On the right of the well deck, the foundation and post for the port side electric baggage crane are visible, because the crane has not yet been installed. (Ioannis Georgiou/Mark Chirnside/Daniel Klistorner/J. Kent Layton collection)

yet *Olympic*'s would enjoy no fewer than three, plus a lift for second-class passengers. First-class passengers had a reading and writing room, lounge, smoke room and veranda cafés, reception room and dining saloon. For the first time on a British liner, an extra-tariff *à la carte* restaurant was included, to provide a wider range of dishes and liberate passengers from the fixed hours of the dining saloon. A gymnasium, Turkish bath suite, swimming pool and squash court completed the facilities. The finished product showed a number of alterations compared to the initial plans of July 1908: the gymnasium was moved to the boat deck; the domed skylight over the first-class smoke room was removed; the second-class smoke room's original location directly beneath it on B-deck was allocated instead to the new restaurant; the dome above the first-class dining saloon was removed; the enormous second-class dining saloon was reduced; the third-class general room, originally spanning the entire width of the ship at the aft end of D-deck was scaled down and then moved; the rather plain first-class staircases were enlarged and given an elegant sweep from deck to deck. There was a marked reduction in third-class capacities which allowed more space for each passenger. And then there was J. Bruce Ismay's request for a change to improve her aesthetic qualities. After he arrived in New York on board White Star's *Oceanic* in June 1909, he observed *Lusitania's* departure: her profile showed a beautiful symmetry with four funnels and *two* masts. Ismay 'decided then and there to add a mainmast to the White Star leviathans, both of which were designed to carry only a foremast.'[5] Although the anecdote may be apocryphal, an additional mast was added to the design. The two ships were intended to be so similar that decisions taken for *Olympic* were to apply equally to her slightly younger sister.

Ismay took a special interest in the new vessels. He 'personally went into all the details' of the porthole and lighting arrangements. Since he admired some of the teak windows fitted on board *Mauretania*, he went so far as to ask Cunard for the working drawings so that a similar design could be used on board *Olympic*. Although close rivals, the two companies co-operated if it was to their mutual benefit. Meanwhile, Harland & Wolff asked Liverpool's Thomas Utley to produce special designs, with three provisos: that they 'would not become obsolete in twenty years' time'; that the portholes for many of the lower first-class staterooms should be 'of immense size'; and 'that under no circumstances would the builders have rectangular holes cut in the shell plating'. While they had the luxury of using large, rectangular windows for the upper decks of the superstructure (the boat, promenade and bridge decks), to ensure the ship's structural integrity only round portholes could be cut in the hull itself. This avoided the problem of stress concentrations at corners.

Olympic would cater for an unprecedented number of first-class passengers. In 1911, it was commonplace even for first-class passengers to share their stateroom with a stranger. Popular demand was rising for greater privacy. *Olympic's* innovations included almost 100 single-berth staterooms. Most first-class staterooms were not outfitted in 'period' décor, but plainly panelled.

However, a considerable number of large 'suites of rooms' and special staterooms amidships on B and C-deck were decorated in different styles from various periods. The long corridors running outside these rooms were framed with pilasters and fielded panels, in contrast to the machined stiles and plain panels along corridors elsewhere in first and second class.

The vast improvements were obvious in comparison with her predecessors such as the 'Big Four'. *Celtic* had a grand total of four 'suites of rooms' with private bathrooms for first-class passengers; *Cedric* had eight; *Baltic* had twelve. It was not until *Adriatic* entered service that, as well as twelve 'suites of rooms'

Left: J.P. Morgan with Lord Pirrie at *Olympic*'s launch. During the course of a dinner in 1908, Morgan conversed with Lord Balfour, then governor of the Bank of Scotland. 'He was cracking up the White Star ships when Balfour asked him if he had travelled in [Cunard's] new ships, and he said no, but he heard that the vibration was terrible and they were most uncomfortable – rattling you to bits.' Morgan's comments prompted one official to ask Vernon Brown, Cunard's agent in New York, if he 'could get any press remarks about the exaggeration of the vibration'. (Author's collection)

with private bathrooms, sixteen ordinary staterooms had these facilities. *Olympic* made an even greater leap forward. Although she carried far more first-class passengers, there were no fewer than sixteen suites with private bathroom facilities and twenty-six bathrooms for ordinary staterooms.

Olympic's second-class dining saloon extended the entire width of the ship, continuing an improvement seen on *Adriatic*, while the smoke room and library were more than comfortable. The previous generation of White Star liners looked inadequate in comparison. *Oceanic*'s second-class smoke room and library combined would have fitted into *Olympic*'s smoke room several times over. Second class enjoyed a vast expanse of deck space, as well as having their own open promenade on the highest deck, the boat deck. Third-class passengers had little to complain about. *Olympic*'s capacity for

Above: *Olympic*'s stern leads the way as she makes the irreversible transition to water. Unlike *Lusitania*, her propellers were not installed prior to launching, but any worries as to her progress were soon dispelled:

> There are so many things which might happen; for example, the vessel might stick on the ways, and have to be forced down into the water, or – a much more rare occurrence – she might on being water borne turn turtle, as did the ill-fated *Principessa Jolanda* when launched from the Società Esercizio Bacini yard at Riva Trigoso, near Spezzia. If, then, there is always anxiety for a vessel, no matter what her size, how much more will there be when a greater weight than has ever before been launched has to be sent down the slip?

According to *The Engineer*: 'For lubricating the ways fifteen tons of pure tallow, five tons of a mixture of train oil and tallow, and three tons of soft soap were employed. Everything went off as smoothly and as easily as though the weight had been less than 7,000 tons instead of 27,000 [sic]...' (Author's collection)

'…The arrangements for stopping her way acted admirably, and in less than twice her length the *Olympic* was brought to a standstill. She was then taken in charge by the four powerful Liverpool tugs, the *Alexandra*, *Brocklebank*, *Formby*, and *Herculaneum*, and escorted to the new wharf to the north of the new graving dock, where she is to be fitted out.' (Ioannis Georgiou/Mark Chirnside/Daniel Klistorner/J. Kent Layton collection)

third-class passengers was about the same as that of the *Majestic* twenty years earlier. Many little details would be appreciated by passengers, right down to the large chairs in the third-class dining saloon which were fitted spaced further apart than on other liners of the period.

★

Olympic and her sister were fairly traditional in their design and construction. Lord Pirrie laid down the length, breadth and general dimensions, as well as the basic hull form and proportions; Alexander Carlisle, chairman of the managing directors and general manager of the shipyard, worked on the complete general arrangements; Thomas Andrews, chief of the design department, was involved closely, taking over Carlisle's duties after his

retirement at the end of June 1910; and Edward Wilding worked on the scientific side of the design process, including the necessary calculations of strength and watertight subdivision. Unlike Cunard, whose liners were designed by their own naval architect, White Star relied on Harland & Wolff. On 16 December 1908 *Olympic*'s keel was laid; *Titanic*'s followed on the last day of March 1909. None of the White Star Line's ships were classed by Lloyd's, but Harland & Wolff were familiar with the classification society's requirements and the steel used was tested to the satisfaction of a Lloyd's surveyor. Although modern high-tensile steel was used in the Cunarders' upper structures to help save weight, it was not for the White Star ships. Thomas Andrews explained that 'the stability of these vessels would be so much greater than that of the *Lusitania* and *Mauretania* that lightness in the upper works was not a vital necessity with them as it had been in the case of these two ships.'

Where necessary, the steel plating was doubled for additional strength along the hull; the rivets holding the ship's plates together were hydraulically driven wherever possible ('a slow and expensive affair, but it was done'); steel rivets being used amidships and iron rivets towards the bow and stern where hand riveting was more appropriate. The watertight bulkheads which extended from one side of the ship to the other, dividing the hull into compartments, were especially strong – well in excess of Lloyd's requirements – and contributed to the ship's strength. Despite their great size, it was originally proposed to dock the ships on a single line of blocks underneath the keel, which required 'special consideration' in Edward Wilding's words.

Although the Board of Trade believed in March 1910 that '*Titanic* and *Olympic* are each to be fitted with 32 boats', the plans Harland & Wolff submitted on 30 June 1910 showed the original fourteen lifeboats and two emergency cutters. Early in June 1911, the shipbuilder told them that an extra 'four collapsible boats with a total cubic capacity of 1,584ft were fitted onboard', making a total of twenty lifeboats. The Welin davits were capable of holding more lifeboats and it was envisaged that regulations might require that in the future, but the new ships comfortably exceeded the existing regulations which had come into effect in 1894. They required larger ships ('over 10,000 tons') to carry a larger number of lifeboats (sixteen under davits 'with a minimum capacity of 5,500 cubic feet'). However, ships had grown considerably by the start of the twentieth century. Nor was a ship's size a reliable guide to the number of people on board in any case, particularly when some liners carried huge numbers of third-class passengers whose accommodation was hardly spacious. The smaller German liner *President Lincoln* complied with American, British and German laws and could carry over 4,100 people, even more than *Olympic* and *Titanic*, but her lifeboat capacity fell short of that by 2,643 persons!

The prime consideration was keeping a damaged vessel afloat through the use of watertight subdivision. As Sir Digby Murray, professional member of the marine department at the Board of Trade and a former White Star commodore, had explained in June 1887:

> The *Britannic* [of 1874] especially has been saved twice by her [watertight] bulkheads; once with two compartments full; this last time with one compartment full. And I need not tell you that there is very great risk to life even in smooth weather the moment you have to lower your boats… I believe you can make ships perfectly safe by [watertight] subdivision of them; I think the *Britannic* has amply proved that.

Cunard's naval architect had considered the question of lifeboat capacity when *Lusitania* and *Mauretania* were being designed. They only carried sixteen lifeboats, but they had ample watertight subdivision and that number was seen as perfectly adequate. At a time when wireless was still relatively new, many vessels did not maintain a twenty-four hour watch or even have wireless apparatus installed, so it was far from certain that help could be summoned immediately. The thought of lowering a ship's passengers and crew into small boats in the middle of the vast, hostile Atlantic Ocean was far from appealing. It was far better to rely on sound construction and watertight subdivision, and even if a vessel was fatally damaged then her safety features would keep her afloat until help arrived. The White Star liner *Republic* did just that after she was involved in a collision in January 1909, remaining afloat for one and a half days until her passengers and crew had been ferried to rescue ships. Had that event turned out differently, perhaps it would have served as a 'wake-up call'. As it was, *Republic's* loss simply confirmed the virtue of prevailing opinion.

By July 1910, in one reporter's words, *Olympic* and *Titanic* were well advanced: 'in addition to their imposing appearance on the stocks, popular

An interesting postcard issued to mark *Olympic's* launch. Alongside a number of minor errors sits the claim that she displaced (or weighed) 66,000 tons. In fact, at her designed load in normal service she displaced 52,310 tons. The error persists to this day. (Author's collection)

THE NEW WHITE STAR LINER "OLYMPIC" AFTER LAUNCHING.

45,000 tons gross register. 66,000 tons displacement. Built by Harland & Wolff, Belfast; launched October 20, 1910. Accommodation 2,500 passengers and a crew of 860. Speed 21 knots. Estimated cost £1,500,000. The "Olympic" is 100 feet longer and 12,500 tons more than the Cunard leviathans, The following are the dimensions, etc., of the great vessel:

Length over all ... ... 882ft. 6in.	Distance from top of funnel to keel ... ... 175ft. 0in.
Breadth over all ... ... 92ft. 6in.	Number of steel decks 11
Breadth over boat deck ... ... 94ft. 0in.	Number of water-tight bulkheads 15
Height from bottom of keel to boat deck ... 97ft. 4in.	Rudder weighs ... ... 100 tons.
Height from bottom of keel to top of captain's	Stern frame, rudder and brackets ... ... 280 tons.
house ... ... 105ft. 7in.	Each anchor ... ... 15 tons.
Height of funnels above casing ... ... 72ft. 0in.	Bronze Propellor ... ... 22 tons.
Height of funnels above boat deck ... ... 81ft. 6in.	Launching weight ... ... 27,000 tons.

Above: *Olympic's* enormous boilers and propelling machinery were lowered into the hull after launch. Although Harland & Wolff were confident of the theoretical benefits of combining two reciprocating engines with a low-pressure turbine, the opportunity arose to test it on a smaller scale before making the final decision. On 30 April 1907 two new ships were ordered which became *Laurentic* and *Megantic*, for use on the Canadian service. *Laurentic* adopted the new concept and was equipped with three propellers, while her sister relied upon reciprocating engines alone and was driven by two, but they would not be completed until 1909.

After White Star had given the 'go ahead' for *Olympic* and her sister on 31 July 1908, whose preliminary design included three propellers driven by the combination machinery, the shipyard and engine works were ordered to proceed 'except with machinery' on 17 September 1908; *Olympic's* keel was laid on 16 December 1908; the shipyard and engine works were ordered to proceed 'with boilers' on 26 February 1909. Meanwhile, *Laurentic* had been launched on 9 September 1908. It was 'generally supposed' in the press that if her engines proved satisfactory then the arrangement would be followed with *Olympic*. She was delivered on 15 April 1909. Her trials seem to have been entirely satisfactory and Harland & Wolff proceeded 'with [the] remainder of machinery' for *Olympic* on 20 April 1909. *Laurentic* made her maiden voyage nine days later. Needless to say, *Olympic's* propelling machinery was on a far greater scale: *Laurentic* required only six smaller double-ended boilers rather than twenty-four larger ones; she was only designed for 16 knots rather than 21 knots; and *Olympic's* engines could develop six times as much horsepower. (*The Engineer*, 1909/Author's collection)

Above: *Olympic* nears completion. Her second funnel is already installed, while the deckhouse for the first-class entrance is clearly visible and deck fixtures such as the Welin lifeboat davits are in place. The enormous funnel in the foreground helps to demonstrate the elliptical shape of the funnels: they were not round. (Mike Poirier collection)

imagination anticipates the important epoch they will mark in the history of British shipbuilding…'

However luxurious the liners were, speed was also important. In order to ensure a competitive schedule *Olympic* was designed to maintain a service speed of 21 knots, with plenty of reserve power to increase speed and make up for any delays she might encounter. No fewer than twenty-four double-ended and five single-ended boilers, with a total of 159 furnaces, were required to supply steam to the engines.

Harland & Wolff opted for the traditional, tried and tested piston-based reciprocating engines to drive the port and starboard propellers. Where they differed from earlier reciprocating engines was in their exceptional size. Another important difference was that they would run in conjunction with a low-pressure steam turbine which drove the central propeller. The turbine was driven by exhaust steam from the reciprocating engines, because it could take advantage of this low-pressure steam even after the reciprocating engines

ENTRANCE TO BELFAST HARBOUR.

were unable to. As a result, the combination arrangement was far more economical than reciprocating engines alone. The reciprocating engines developed 15,000 indicated horsepower at 75 revolutions each minute, but the turbine ran much faster and developed 16,000 shaft horsepower at 165 revolutions.[*] Although only 46,000 horsepower was required for a speed of 21 knots, the propelling machinery could develop around 59,000 horsepower.

The size and power of the reciprocating engines was extraordinary. 'I do not think many people who have not been there, realise the enormous power that there is got from the steam pressure in these engines; they move comparatively slowly even when at full power, and the power behind them

Titanic is visible in the distance on her slipway; in the foreground, part of the graving dock can be seen, with the pump house largely out of the picture; and further behind the photographer's vantage point lay the outfitting wharf. Although it was opened in 1911, it was not until 20 May 1915 that the dock was named the Thompson Graving Dock by the Lord Lieutenant of Ireland. Among those in attendance was the Right Honourable Robert Thompson, chairman of the Belfast Harbour Commissioners. (Author's collection)

---

[*] The measure of power output for a piston-based reciprocating engine was 'indicated horsepower' (IHP), whereas a turbine engine's output was measured in 'shaft horsepower' (SHP).

Titanic's centre anchor – weighing 15½ tons – leaves Messrs Noah Hingley & Sons Ltd at Netherton, Dudley, for the 2-mile journey to the town's railway station. Although dated Monday 1 May 1911, the people in their 'Sunday best' indicate it was taken the previous day. The White Star Line were frustrated that their name was not mentioned in newspaper reports. It was 'ascribed entirely to the difficulty of controlling irresponsible press notices in connection with the details of a vessel of such world wide interest.' The anchor was conveyed to Belfast via a cross-channel steamer, but the rate charged was 'exceptionally low, and was not a paying transaction' according to the London & North Western Railway District Goods Manager's Office at Wolverhampton. When *Britannic*'s anchor needed to be conveyed several years later, the price went up accordingly: it was heavier, at 16 tons, although the overall dimensions were kept the same.

In October 1911, the manufacturer wrote to Harland & Wolff requesting a photograph of *Olympic* for their boardroom: 'We naturally take a great interest in this magnificent pair of vessels, and are proud of the fact that we have supplied you with the cable and anchor outfits for both…' (Jonathan Smith collection)

is, I think I am correct in stating, larger than the power behind the biggest rolling mills in the world. That is, the biggest mills that are used anywhere for the rolling of steel plates, as distinct from the forging of armour plates,' stated Harland & Wolff's Edward Wilding in spring 1912. One of *Olympic*'s reciprocating engines on its own was more powerful than both of *Adriatic*'s engines combined. Future liners would be equipped with turbine engines and so *Olympic*'s engine room appeared all the more impressive as the enormous crankshafts plunged up and down, driving the propellers at a maximum speed of over 80 revolutions per minute.

★

Another impressive sight greeted spectators at Belfast on the morning of 20 October 1910: 'admiring crowds were gazing with awe at the leviathan which reared her gigantic hull far above their heads'. *Olympic* was launched shortly before 11 a.m.:

Her sharp bow, beautiful lines and clean run from stem to stern suggest speed, her tremendous weight, rigidity and strength indicate stability, and like the *Oceanic* eleven years ago she may proudly claim the title of 'Queen of the Seas'.

There is something awe-inspiring in the proportions of the *Olympic*. She bulks largely in one's imagination, and suggests marvellous developments in future transmarine operations. Moderate terms and comparison between this gigantic creation of shipbuilder's genius and her predecessors fail of their purpose when applied to such a ship, and the mind is almost staggered by her wonderful size, her general dimensions internally, and the luxury and completeness of her appointments. She is the apotheosis of skill as applied to the dominion of the ocean, and really dominates and triumphs over all previous achievements.

The *Southampton Times* called her a 'wonderful demonstration of the rapid strides that have been made in modern shipbuilding' and enthused 'nothing has been left to chance; everything has been carefully thought out and

A FAMILY RESEMBLANCE

Top left: *Laurentic*'s first-class grand staircase; **Top right:** the ship's first-class smoke room; **Bottom left:** *Adriatic*'s first-class lounge; **Bottom right:** *Oceanic*'s first-class library, showing the bookcase. (Author's collection)

One of the most enduring myths about *Olympic* and her sister is that their interiors were uniquely grand and original. There is no doubt that first-class passengers enjoyed a range of facilities that were unprecedented at the time they entered service, from the spacious reception room and other public rooms, to the squash court, swimming pool, gymnasium and Turkish and electric bath establishment. Passengers could take in the gorgeous expanse of the forward grand staircase, whose upper levels marked one of the finest interior spaces on any liner. The spaciousness of their enclosed promenades and open decks was not matched by any other vessel, while *Olympic*'s lavish first-class suites won widespread praise and affection right into the 1930s.

Titanic even introduced the first two private promenade decks to go to sea. However, in many regards they shared a family resemblance with earlier White Star liners built by Harland & Wolff, albeit on a much larger and improved scale. (James Miller, designer of *Lusitania*'s interiors, asked for an introduction to J. Bruce Ismay as he was keen to undertake work on White Star's ships, but evidently the company did not depart from their existing plans.) *Olympic* and *Titanic* avoided the hideous grandiosity on board many of their German rivals but, while it is right to avoid modern-day myth-making, it is necessary to appreciate them for what they were. Their décor made for a more pleasing visual effect, while their accommodation was – in many respects – unparalleled when they entered service.

Above: *Olympic* lies at Berth 44, dressed prior to her maiden voyage. Her impressive profile was admired by many. At a reception for local dignitaries after her arrival at Southampton, Harold Sanderson, one of the White Star Line's directors, commented:

> Some of those present who had read descriptions of the vessel in some of the papers might have been disappointed at not finding the motor racing track, the skating rink, the botanical gardens and the zoological gardens, but even they would not be so disappointed as the motorists, the professional skaters, the head gardeners and the lion tamers who had applied to the White Star Line for appointments which they had not been able to give them.

(Mark Chirnside/Günter Bäbler/Daniel Klistorner collection)

Left: From the left: Philip Franklin, then vice-president of IMM; Charles Burlingham, who represented the White Star Line at the limitation of liability hearings that followed the *Titanic* disaster; and J. Bruce Ismay, photographed in 1912. One of the most well-known studio portraits of J. Bruce Ismay was actually taken in 1899, when he was in his mid-thirties. Consequently, he appears much older in this image, and celebrated his fiftieth birthday in December 1912. (Library of Congress, Prints and Photographs Division)

Right: On 9 June 1911, *Olympic*'s commander, Captain Edward John Smith, and Lord William James Pirrie, of Harland & Wolff, stand next to the gymnasium on the starboard side of the boat deck. Born in Hanley on 27 January 1850, Smith joined the White Star Line shortly after his thirtieth birthday. He was briefly in command of *Republic* in 1887 and *Baltic* the following year, but it was not until he joined *Cufic* as her commander in December 1888 that he put his days as an officer behind him permanently. By July 1895, he was in charge of the prestigious *Majestic* and he remained until June 1904, save for a brief period when he commanded the old *Germanic* in 1902–03. Smith took charge of the new *Baltic*, the largest vessel afloat, in June 1904 and then joined *Adriatic* for her maiden voyage in May 1907. Four years later, he took command of *Olympic* and then *Titanic*. J. Bruce Ismay stated that the White Star Line held Smith in 'entire and absolute confidence'. He dropped three years from his age when he signed on as *Titanic*'s captain, stating that he was fifty-nine.

Pirrie joined Harland & Wolff as an apprentice in 1862 and was admitted to the partnership in 1874. He became a peer in 1906. Following Sir Edward Harland's death in 1895 and Gustav Wolff's retirement in 1906, he took charge of the shipyard and oversaw a programme of expansion. His career was 'one of the most notable among those of the great captains of industry' according to *The Shipbuilder* in 1911. After his death abroad in 1924, his body was carried home by *Olympic*, his favourite ship. (Topical Press Agency/Getty Images)

skilfully planned, and in many cases completely revised, down to the most minute details…' One reporter wrote: 'She was not built to fail; a higher destiny awaits her'.

Seven months passed, while her machinery was installed and interiors outfitted: a remarkable accomplishment for the largest liner in the world. Following *Olympic*'s two days of sea trials at the end of May 1911 and *Titanic*'s launch on 31 May 1911, *Olympic* left Belfast for Liverpool, where she would be opened for public inspection prior to her voyage to Southampton.

OLYMPIC'S MAIDEN VOYAGE

During the early hours of 3 June 1911, *Olympic* arrived at Southampton. 'The visitors who thronged to the dock from the early hours of the morning were greatly impressed with the biggest ship the world has ever known.' Her commander and officers had plenty of work to do in preparation for the maiden voyage, but they were already 'well pleased with the manner in which she performed' on the voyage from Liverpool.

Around noon on Wednesday, 14 June 1911, *Olympic* left Southampton 'in beautiful weather'; by 7.30 p.m. she was at Cherbourg and, after two hours, on her way to Queenstown. She was late in arriving, dropping anchor around 2.30 p.m. 'A number of travellers who joined her at Southampton and Cherbourg for the short run to Queenstown were unbounded in their praise for the magnificence of every detail of the mighty liner', the *Cork Examiner* gushed. 'She came right into the inner harbour of Queenstown today, and notwithstanding her great depth of water and enormous size, she manoeuvred

Right: Thomas Andrews was born on 7 February 1873 and named after his father. He left school at sixteen and entered Harland & Wolff as a premium apprentice, rising rapidly through the ranks. By 1905, he had been promoted to chief of the design department at the age of thirty-two; in March 1907 he also became a managing director of the firm. When Alexander Carlisle, chairman of the managing directors and general manager of the yard, retired at the end of June 1910, Andrews took over his duties.

Andrews married Helen Reilly in June 1908 and their first child, Elizabeth Law Barbour Andrews, was born two years later. Politically, Andrews was a unionist and advocated 'moderate social reform on lines carefully designed to encourage thrift, temperance and endeavour'.

Following the success of *Olympic*'s maiden voyage, he worked hard to make further improvements to *Titanic* and, shortly before she left Belfast on 2 April 1912, Andrews showed a number of friends around the ship. After the sinking, a memorial service was held in his home town of Comber (10 miles to the south-east of Belfast) on 21 April 1912. It was conducted by Reverend Thomas Dunkerley, who had known him since he was six years old and watched Andrews become an adult who was 'intelligent, industrious, earnest, enterprising and diligent to the point of strenuousness', attaining his position at Harland & Wolff through 'sheer toil and ability'.

His father and mother both outlived him. His older brother, John Miller Andrews (1871–1956), served as Northern Ireland's prime minister from 1940–43; his younger brother James Andrews (1877–1951) became Lord Chief Justice in 1937; and Willie Andrews (1886–1966) was well known in cricket. His sister Nina (1874–1930) was widowed when her husband, Lawrence A. Hind, was killed in action at the Somme in 1916. Andrews' widow Helen (1881–1966) married Henry Harland in 1917. Andrews' daughter was killed in a car accident in 1973. (George Behe collection)

S.S. OLYMPIC LEAVING SOUTHAMPTON.

Left: One of a series of similar postcards shows *Olympic* leaving Southampton, perhaps on her maiden voyage. The tugs and other small craft are dwarfed by the largest liner in the world. (Ioannis Georgiou/Daniel Klistorner/Mark Chirnside collection)

Above: A very early view of *Olympic* – taken on her maiden voyage – shows her impressive profile. She appears to be coming into New York, with the New Jersey shoreline across the Hudson River. Perhaps she is off Quarantine, waiting for clearance to proceed to her pier. (Mark Chirnside/Daniel Klistorner collection)

Right: Passengers line her decks as *Olympic* is brought into Pier 59, New York. (Author's collection)

It is popularly believed that *Lusitania* was more popular with the travelling public than her sister. Although this was true for her early years, in fact *Mauretania* surpassed her in 1909–10 and continued to do better thereafter; before the war she carried a higher total number of passengers than *Lusitania*, with a higher average passenger list. (Author's collection)

Above: *Olympic* alongside her New York pier. For the workmen who climbed her funnels, a fear of heights was far from desirable. (Ioannis Georgiou/Mark Chirnside/Daniel Klistorner/J. Kent Layton collection)

under her triple screws with as much ease as a motor launch'. She had 'a majesty and grace of movement which was the admiration of all who beheld her'.

Olympic left Queenstown later that afternoon and passed Daunt's Rock, which marked the start of the crossing to New York, but it was already clear she would fulfil the hopes embodied in her. 'The amazing steadiness of the ship was a frequent source of comment. For two or three days… the most frequent enquiry was "Have the engines stopped?" But the engines had not stopped, the screws were still plowing [sic] up the foam', wrote one observer for the *New York Times*. The squash court proved so popular that the White Star Line had to limit games to half an hour.

Thomas Andrews made a large number of notes for improvements, down to the smallest details: the notice boards at the ship's stern ('Warning This Vessel Has Triple Screws Keep Clear of Blades') needed to be permanently fitted rather than stowed away after use, as it damaged the paintwork; eleven extra four-seat tables were required in the *à la carte* restaurant which had proved more popular than anticipated; additional furniture was needed for the 'most popular room in the first-class passenger accommodation' (the reception room); and sponge holders needed to be fitted in the private bathrooms where they had been omitted. Captain Smith recommended to him the fitting of 'protective windows with round bulls eye lights' on the windows of the bridge front 'as in *Adriatic*'; linoleum tiles did not need to be fitted in Smith's sitting room as a full carpet had been provided; and, to prevent an uncomfortable

Right: *Olympic*'s huge size meant that the White Star Line and IMM had to go to considerable efforts to improve the New York docking facilities. 'In the foreground is shown the temporary 100-foot extension of the pier which is built of open piling with free passageway for the tidal flow. In the same basin with the *Olympic* is the *Finland*, 580 feet in length. In the adjoining basin is the 704-foot [sic] *Oceanic*...' (*Scientific American*, 1911/Author's collection)

Below: If one of the White Star Line's express steamers arrived at New York in the evening, whether she was early or late, passengers were able to remain on board overnight so that they would not be inconvenienced. A series of 'Notes for the Convenience of First Class Passengers' were issued with the White Star Line's compliments for *Adriatic*'s maiden voyage in May 1907. The arrangements remained in place during *Olympic*'s service. (Author's collection)

LANDING AT NEW YORK.

Should the steamer arrive at the New York Wharf after 8 p.m., passengers have the option of remaining on board overnight and landing after breakfast on the following morning.

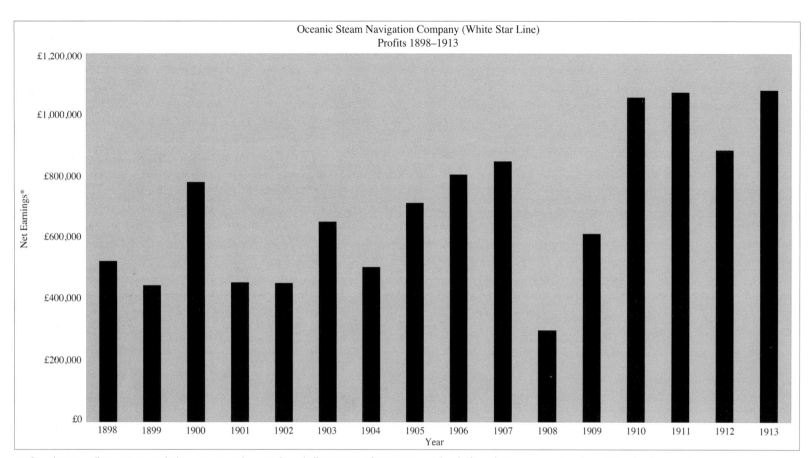

Oceanic Steam Navigation Company (White Star Line)
Profits 1898–1913

'*After charging all outgoings, including repairs and renewals and all expenses of management, but before charging interest and providing for depreciation.'

Although the White Star Line enjoyed good and bad years over the period from 1898 to 1913, its profits were on a rising trend as the company gained strength. They narrowly reached a new high in 1913 and the war years would see dramatic increases. (Author's collection)

draft in one of the stairways used by stewards and stewardesses, he noted a 'wood bulkhead with sliding doors be fitted at foot of stairs.'

During the course of the voyage, the speed was gradually increased. Her final day's run of 548 miles was achieved with five boilers remaining unlit, yet she averaged over 22 knots with plenty of power in reserve. Her coal consumption was significantly lower than anticipated and she arrived in New York with 1,300 tons remaining in her bunkers. She completed the crossing in five days, fifteen hours and two minutes at an average speed of 21.43 knots.[6] *Olympic*'s performance had been superb. When she came into her berth that Wednesday morning of 21 June 1911, her pilot, Julius Adler,

commented: 'She handles like a catboat,' saying, 'She answered the shadow of a touch upon her steering gear.' Captain Smith wore 'a smile that couldn't come off' and passengers 'were loud in their praises of the ship'. The *Syracuse Herald* noted that she docked at 8.50 a.m.:

All the way up the bay from the Narrows a fleet of small craft had shrieked a noisy welcome to the new giantess on her first trip into New York harbour.

The tops of high buildings and windows in the skyscrapers were crowded, watching the progress of the leviathan as she slowly made her way up stream. Vessels alongside resembled pygmies…

Ismay cabled Lord Pirrie: '*Olympic* is a marvel, and has given unbounded satisfaction. Once again accept my warmest and most sincere congratulations.'[7] Like Andrews, he had noted a few minor deficiencies: although the ship was 'practically quiet' even at high speed, the bed springs were 'too "springy", this, in conjunction with the spring mattresses, accentuated the pulsation in the ship to such an extent as to seriously interfere with the passengers sleeping.' He wanted to arrange for lath bottoms to be fitted before the next voyage. Alongside a number of minor points, he suggested that the first-class staterooms on B-deck could be extended out to the ship's side on *Titanic*, at the expense of the enclosed promenade deck.

Olympic's 489 first-class, 263 second-class and 564 third-class passengers totalled 1,316: more than four times higher than the number her running mate *Oceanic* had brought into New York the previous week. The first-class figure represented a westbound record, but she was soon to set an eastbound record as well. When *Olympic* left New York on 28 June 1911, she carried 736 first, 491 second and 1,052 third-class passengers: a grand total of 2,279. 'Leaving New York on the return voyage, the *Olympic* will steam about twenty-one knots the first day,' Ismay told one reporter, 'and then gradually be increased until the maximum speed of the engines is attained, and then we shall have a good idea of what the ship can do.' After two leisurely days, she increased her speed and maintained between 22.5 and 23 knots for the remainder of the voyage. It was reported that the cost of the round trip would come to $175,000 (£35,000), with passenger receipts at $225,000 (£45,000); this would have generated a healthy profit if the figures were accurate.

On her second westbound departure from Southampton, Lord Pirrie and J.P. Morgan were among the 514 first-class passengers. Symbolising the optimism of many, Pirrie had said publicly that there was 'no structural reason why 100,000 ton ships should not be built'. Perhaps he was proud when the second day's run of 560 miles was posted, showing an average speed of over 22.5 knots. Thomas Andrews and Edward Wilding endeavoured 'with the aid of Schlick's instruments' to 'measure the amplitude and frequency' of vibration in various parts of the ship. They found that it was noticeably greater with the reciprocating engines running at 80 to 81 revolutions, compared to 76 to 77 revolutions. Vibration was more noticeable in the vicinity of the first-class smoke room, the centre of the ship and the forward end of the superstructure. Andrews would make some notes for localised

Olympic's proud officers. Standing, left to right: Purser Hugh McElroy; Third Officer Henry Cater; Second Officer Robert Hume; Fourth Officer David Alexander; Sixth Officer Harold Holehouse. Seated, left to right: Fifth Officer Adolphus Tulloch; Chief Officer Joseph Evans; Captain Edward John Smith and First Officer William Murdoch. After the maiden voyage, Evans was replaced as chief officer by Henry Wilde. (George Behe collection)

modifications to reduce it further on *Titanic*. In general, however, *Olympic* was remarkably free of vibration, which plagued earlier German express liners, as well as Cunard's *Lusitania* and *Mauretania* when they entered service. On the eastbound return crossing, she increased her best day's run as she maintained an average of 23.24 knots with the current in her favour.

Cunard were looking for ideas for their planned new liner, *Aquitania*, and so Leonard Peskett, their naval architect, came on board to observe *Olympic*'s third eastbound crossing. He was impressed 'with the superabundance of promenade deck space'. The boat deck, in particular the roof above the first-class lounge, was used by some passengers for deck games, but deckchairs were not allowed there. Instead, they were on A-deck, which was also popular with passengers taking in the sea air; in contrast, B-deck 'was deserted, and never at any time during the voyage' was a passenger seen there. He was particularly impressed by the decoration of the *á la carte* restaurant, but criticised other public rooms and felt that the first-class 'en suite and special cabins are overdone in detail and garish in decoration'. The squash court 'was patronised and monopolised by about sixteen individuals who were continually playing during the hours the place was open.' He made many recommendations for *Aquitania*, including such things as the ship's coaling gear; the desirability of having a maids' and valets' dining saloon; and installing emergency electric dynamos high above the waterline as on *Olympic*.

Olympic's performance had given rise to some discussions between J. Bruce Ismay and Philip Franklin, vice-president of IMM. After her second westbound arrival in New York, she had arrived at the Ambrose Channel lightship at 10.08 p.m., remaining at Quarantine before docking the next morning. Franklin suggested: 'I do hope, and strongly recommend, that next voyage you allow her to dock here on Tuesday evening, as it will materially assist in advertising the steamer, and help us very much in turning her round, and give everybody on shipboard a better chance, and I am sure it would please the passengers.' Ismay acknowledged Franklin's letter, agreeing that it would help prepare the ship for her return as well as pleasing the passengers, but he was far from keen on 'the miseries of a night landing in New York'. He felt it would create uncertainty for passengers, who would rather know for definite that they would arrive on Wednesday. In the end, Ismay said that he would 'not allow my individual feelings to stand in the way' if discussions with Lord Pirrie, Captain Smith and Chief Engineer Bell favoured the

suggestion. Smith was instructed on 11 August 1911 'to go full speed when on the short track, subject to your considering it prudent and in the interests of safe navigation to do so. This instruction applies to both the eastbound and westbound voyages.' (Her first three voyages were on the longer Southern Track, but the shorter Northern Track, which was in force from 24 August to 14 January each year, could reduce the crossing time by four or five hours for a ship of *Olympic*'s speed.)

When *Olympic* arrived in New York for the fourth time, she docked on Tuesday evening and 'the baggage was all gotten out promptly considering the very large quantity, and the cabin passengers were well away before 11.30 [p.m.], and everybody seemed to be well satisfied and there were no complaints,' according to Franklin on 7 September 1911. Westbound passenger lists at that time of year were always good, when passengers returned to America from Europe, and *Olympic* was playing her part.

Notes

1   Strouse, Jean, *Morgan: American Financier* (Perennial: 2000) p.480.

2   Oldham, Wilton J., *The Ismay Line* (*The Journal of Commerce*: 1961) p.167.

3   Bäbler, Günter, 'The Dinner at Lord Pirrie's in Summer 1907: Just a Legend?' *Titanic Post,* June 2000, vol.32, p.16.

4   The second series of bonds was not issued for several years. By July 1914, the White Star Line had decided to increase the authorised total to £3,375,000 rather than £2,500,000. They issued a further £1,500,000 worth of bonds paying the same interest. For a comprehensive outline, see the relevant appendix in *The 'Olympic' Class Ships: Olympic Titanic Britannic* (The History Press: 2011).

5   Cooke, Anthony. '*Olympic* and *Titanic*: How Many Masts?', *Sea Lines* 2006, issue 42, p.32. An extremely interesting article. (See also Harris, James. 'Letter to editor' *Atlantic Daily Bulletin*, 2006. I appreciate David Hill's assistance.) My own additional research into the dates and departure times, as well as Ismay's travels, all support the facts reported.

6   Chirnside, Mark, and Halpern, Sam, '*Olympic* and *Titanic*: Maiden Voyage Mysteries', *Voyage*, 2007, pp.115–25.

7   Oldham, *Op. cit.* p.175.

2

A RUN OF BAD LUCK

THE *HAWKE* COLLISION

On 20 September 1911, the day started out promisingly. *Olympic*'s first-class passenger numbers had risen with every crossing she made from Southampton: – from 489 on her maiden voyage to 718 on her fourth – and now a reported 732 were booked for her fifth westbound crossing. The *Southampton Times* noted: 'the company's officials were congratulating themselves on the fact that another record had been created by the vessel, in that she had on board the largest number of first-class passengers which had ever left an English port in one ship.' It is popularly believed that third-class passengers made the ship pay her way. In fact, first-class ticket receipts were invariably higher and, with some dubbing her the 'millionaires' ship', *Olympic* was earning considerable revenues. But the day marked the start of a chain of horrendous bad luck.

The weather was fine and clear, with a west-south-westerly breeze, when *Olympic* left the dock at 11.20 a.m. She was under the command of a compulsory pilot, George Bowyer, who was on the bridge with Captain Smith. Quartermaster Albert Haines was at the ship's wheel on the open bridge; Fourth Officer David Alexander was operating the telegraphs which relayed engine order commands from the bridge; Sixth Officer Harold Holehouse was recording orders for the ship's log; Chief Officer Henry Wilde was on the forecastle deck at the bow; Second Officer Robert Hume was in the crow's nest; Fifth Officer Adolphus Tulloch was at the conning tower above the first-class lounge which housed the standard compass; and First Officer Murdoch was on the poop deck at the stern.

Proceeding down Southampton Water, *Olympic* needed to execute a reverse 'S'-shaped turn around the western end of the Bramble Bank, before proceeding through the deep waters of the eastern channel into Spithead and then past the Isle of Wight. She slowed from about 17.5 to 11 or 12 knots to make the turn, with the aid of her engines, and after coming out of the final turn at 12.43 p.m. her engines were ordered 'full ahead'. The turbine was brought into operation a minute later and she began to work up to a reduced speed (for coastal waters) of 20 knots. Captain Smith observed the naval cruiser HMS *Hawke* 'almost half a mile' away. She was 'drawing up on our starboard beam' about one or two cables (200 to 400 yards) from *Olympic*'s side as both vessels headed into Spithead; Smith thought 'the distance was perfectly safe and gave no cause for anxiety'. He described: 'For an appreciable time we seemed to run about even [in] speed… Then we gathered speed, drew ahead a little, or she [*Hawke*] dropped astern…'

George Bowyer walked back from the port side of the bridge and Captain Smith drew his attention to an alarming development. Bowyer 'saw her [*Hawke*] swinging very rapidly' *towards* the side of *Olympic*. The two men 'wondered what she was up to'. To Smith, *Hawke* seemed to be deliberately turning in: 'It was an inconceivable manoeuvre,' he thought. He assumed *Hawke*'s commander might be trying to pass behind *Olympic*'s stern. Bowyer believed 'it was rather tricky' and told Smith: 'If she is going to strike, sir, let me know in time, so as I can put the helm hard over to port [turn *Olympic* to starboard].'

'Is she going to strike, sir?' Bowyer shouted.

'Yes,' Smith called back. 'She is going to strike us in the stern.' Haines spun the wheel hard over and *Olympic* began to respond.

Hawke's commander, William Blunt, judged that she was 150 yards from *Olympic*: 'Not dangerous… I have been a great deal closer in a fleet, but it was precious uncomfortable.' He thought the two ships 'were nearly as possible bridge to bridge'. He had previously ordered a slight course adjustment to give *Olympic* more room, but it was soon clear that a dangerous situation had developed. *Hawke*'s bow was moving to port 'not in the ordinary way of a swing, but what I should call a swerve':

> I called down the voice pipe, which is level with my chest, 'What are you doing? Port, port, hard aport'; the words were hardly out of my mouth before I quite realised, with the increasing velocity of this swerve, that no helm the ship could carry was ever going to take her to starboard, and I gave the order 'stop port [engine]; full astern starboard'. At the same moment that I gave the order

I heard the report from the quartermaster 'helm is jambed [sic]'. When I gave the order to 'Stop port; full astern starboard', I sprang to the port ladder which led down to the bridge because, from that point, I can see my telegraphs…The moment the report reached me 'helm is jambed', I jumped from top to bottom and gave the order 'full astern both'. Screws without helm, or helm without screws, was not going to stop her.

Blunt operated the port telegraph himself and then checked that Lieutenant Bashford had rung 'full astern' on the starboard telegraph. When he felt vibration, he believed the engines were running astern and *Hawke*'s speed was being 'materially lessened'. It was too late. *Hawke* smashed into *Olympic*'s side and 'turned right round like a [spinning] top'.

Colonel Sexton White, the general manager of Armstrong, Whitworth & Co.'s shipyard, was on board *Olympic* with his daughter. He took an interest in *Hawke* while they enjoyed the fine weather. They were standing on the

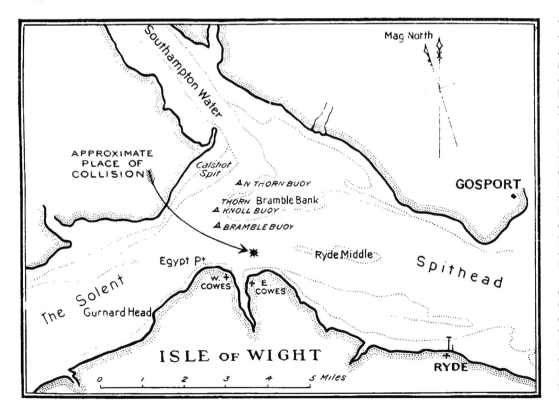

The *Journal of Commerce* published a map depicting the area where the collision took place. It gives an approximate idea and helps to visualise *Olympic*'s manoeuvres. Her speed was reduced to 11 or 12 knots as she passed the North Thorn Buoy at 12.37 p.m.; the pilot, George Bowyer, ordered an easy turn to port, assisted by the slowing of the port engine, to enter the Thorn Channel just before arriving at the Thorn Knoll Buoy at 12.40 p.m.; then, in Bowyer's words, 'as we proceeded and got about two-thirds of the way from the Thorn Knoll to the West Bramble Buoy, I gave orders to blow two blasts [on the whistle], a starboard helm signal, to let the cruiser [*Hawke*] know I was on the starboard helm [turning to port], and that I was bound for the eastern passage. I then stopped the port engine, and went half speed astern on the port, and then proceeded on for a few yards, and went full speed astern on the port to make a short turn round the West Bramble' at 12.43 p.m.

Olympic was then straightened up on the necessary course to proceed down the eastern channel. Fifth Officer Adolphus Tulloch, at the ship's standard compass, checked his reference paper and confirmed *Olympic* was exactly on course ('South 59° East' by the compass) before pressing three bells to notify the bridge. Her engines were ordered 'full ahead' and the turbine brought into operation a minute later as she gathered speed. (Author's collection)

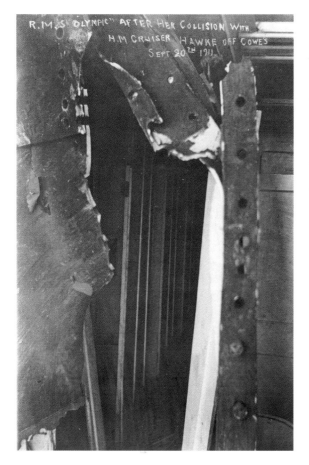

Left: Looking through the damaged shell plating into the third-class accommodation. It was fortunate that the collision occurred at lunchtime. A number of staterooms were damaged on G, F, E and D-deck ('E deck. Woodwork and fittings in rooms Nos 145 and 151 damaged and destroyed, remainder of rooms from frames 103 to 139 damaged…') If they had been occupied, there could easily have been serious injuries or deaths. (Author's collection)

Above: An external view of the damage being inspected at Southampton. Harland & Wolff had to undertake temporary repairs to patch up the hole before *Olympic* could return to the shipyard for permanent repairs. (Author's collection)

starboard side of the promenade deck, near the first-class entrance, when he assumed *Hawke* was going to pass behind *Olympic*'s stern and so turned to cross over to the port side. His daughter cried out, 'She has struck us.' White did not feel any shock, but when he turned back and looked to starboard he saw '*Hawke* recovering from a heavy roll, and gradually her bows being twisted forward and in the direction of the *Olympic*, the vessels were then disengaged.'

Olympic's chief engineer, Robert Fleming, was standing on the top platform in the main engine room when he felt a slight shock. He headed down to the middle platform. As he descended, he 'noticed the starboard engine' – which had been running at about 60–65 revolutions per minute – 'pulled up… just for a moment, and then cleared itself'. *Hawke*, dropping back, had fouled *Olympic*'s starboard propeller. Before he got to the bottom

platform, the telegraph had signalled 'stop' and the engines were soon halted. On the bridge, Holehouse recorded in the rough copy of the deck log: '12.46 [p.m.]. Struck on starboard quarter by HM ship.' Then, a minute later: 'Warning bell rung, watertight doors closed from bridge. 12.47 [p.m.] Stop [engines] and as required…'

It was soon clear the voyage would have to be abandoned. As the *Southampton Times* put it: 'The White Star Line stand to lose heavily. The very fact that the vessel remains "off duty" for some time involves a loss greater than the ordinary man in the street has any idea of.' The *New York Times* remarked on the ship's safety features. They had 'changed what in other days would almost certainly have been an appalling disaster into mere inconvenience for the passengers' and a monetary loss for the shipping line:

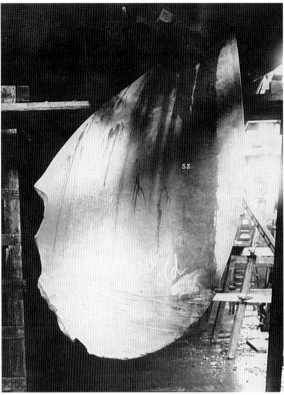

Far left: Once in dry dock, the damage was visible in its entirety, in an inverted pear shape with holes above and below the waterline. At the bottom of the image, part of the plating can be seen curving outwards again, towards the starboard propeller shaft. (National Archives, United Kingdom)

Left: One of the starboard propeller's blades, chipped and scraped as a result of coming into contact with *Hawke*. (National Archives)

Below left: *Olympic*'s first eastbound crossing after the *Hawke* collision. In August 1911, Messrs Ismay, Imrie & Co. (the White Star Line's managers) sent a memo to their New York offices. It included a timetable showing her arrival and departure times if she was on the shorter Northern Track and averaged 22.5 knots, which envisaged her leaving New York at 2 p.m. on 2 December 1911, arriving at Plymouth at 7 a.m., Cherbourg at 2 p.m. and then Southampton at 8 p.m. on 8 December 1911 ('excellent arrival times'). Although the departure date changed, the timetable proved remarkably similar to her actual performance. (Daniel Klistorner collection)

WHITE STAR ROYAL MAIL TRIPLE-SCREW STEAMER "OLYMPIC."
COMMANDER E. J. SMITH, R.D., R.N.R.

ABSTRACT OF LOG.

NEW YORK TO SOUTHAMPTON, VIA PLYMOUTH AND CHERBOURG.
VOYAGE NO. 5, EAST, DECEMBER 9, 1911.
AMBROSE CHANNEL LIGHT VESSEL ABEAM, DECEMBER 9, AT 2.26 P.M. DEPARTURE.

DATE	WIND	LAT. LONG.	MILE.	REMARKS.
10	NW.	41,20 63,55	462	CALM TO LIGHT NW. WINDS, SMOOTH SEA
11	SW. & W'LY	44,10 52,46	527	LIGHT SW. TO GENTLE W'LY. WINDS, SMOOTH SEA
12	NW.	47,27 41,11	518	MOD. TO STRONG NW. WINDS, MOD. TO ROUGH SEA
13	NW. & W'LY	49,32 23,26	522	MOD. TO STRONG NW. & W'LY. WINDS, ROUGH SEA
14	N'LY.	49,55 14,58	523	LIGHT N'LY. TO MOD. SW. WINDS, MOD. SEA
			422	TO EDDYSTONE LIGHT HOUSE

DISTANCE 2974   AVERAGE SPEED 22·487 KNOTS.
ARRIVED 15TH, AT 7.42 A.M. PASSAGE 5 DAYS 12 HOURS 16 MINUTES.

The *Hawke*, it must be remembered, is especially designed for the purpose, among others, of sinking ships by ramming into them, and to do it without harm to herself. Yet she ran into the *Olympic* involuntarily in just about the way, and probably at about the same speed, in and at which she would have rammed a hostile vessel, and she came out of the encounter the worse hurt of the two.

Olympic anchored in Osbourne Bay, returning to Southampton on one engine the next day for temporary repairs. On 4 October 1911, she left for Belfast, where she arrived two days later for dry-docking in the only dock large enough for her. By 22 November 1911 she was back at Southampton, thanks to some strenuous efforts by Harland & Wolff. They also took the opportunity to adjust *Olympic*'s port and starboard propellers to improve her speed and efficiency. Similar adjustments would be made to *Titanic*.

Meanwhile, the company were embroiled in a legal battle. The Royal Navy's own enquiry had interviewed *Hawke*'s officers and crew, before concluding that *Olympic* was solely to blame. White Star disagreed and, with

Left: Francis Carruthers, ship surveyor to the Board of Trade, reported *Titanic*'s sea trials:

The trials consisted of running from slow up to full-speed ahead, manoeuvring with the turbine cut out, going astern and swinging the vessel at full speed ahead with the helm hard over to test the steering gear. After the trials the vessel was brought back to Belfast Lough and the port and starboard anchors dropped and hove up again, all the tests proving satisfactory the vessel sailed for Southampton on the evening of the 2nd…

(*L'Illustration*, 1912/Author's collection, courtesy Daniel Klistorner)

Below left: *Titanic*'s gymnasium equipment included a rowing machine and exercise bicycle. The appliances, originally designed by Swedish doctor Gustav Zander, were ordered from Rossel, Schwarz & Co. in Wiesbaden, Germany. (*L'Illustration*, 1912/Author's collection, courtesy Daniel Klistorner)

Below: The tables in *Titanic*'s starboard veranda café were all square, rather than the mixture of round and square tables on *Olympic*. (*L'Illustration*, 1912/Author's collection, courtesy Daniel Klistorner)

each suing the other, the suits were heard together. Their argument was that *Hawke* was an overtaking vessel, so that her duty ('under the Article of the King's Regulations, which corresponds with Article 24 of the Regulations for Preventing Collisions at Sea') was to keep out of *Olympic*'s way; the naval side argued that the two vessels were crossing, under Article 19 of the regulations, so that *Olympic* was required to keep out of the way of *Hawke*. The issues were complex. *Hawke* had been proceeding at over 15 knots, which was slower than *Olympic*'s normal speed. However, *Olympic* was accelerating for three or four minutes after she had completed the turn, so that her speed increased until it equalled and then surpassed *Hawke*'s.

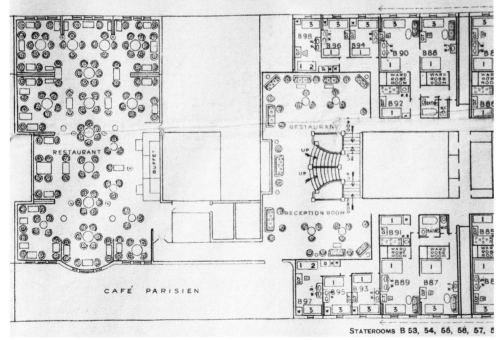

STATEROOMS B 53, 54, 55, 56, 57, 5

Left: A late addition to *Titanic*'s design was the Café Parisien, which did not appear on first-class accommodation plans in December 1911. It was previously listed as a promenade. The windows of the *á la carte* restaurant on the left overlooked the charming French café, while the windows on the right permitted a fine view of the sea. (*L'Illustration*, 1912/Author's collection, courtesy Daniel Klistorner)

Below left: *Titanic*'s *á la carte* restaurant. *Olympic*'s restaurant proved a great success and so *Titanic*'s was expanded and a reception room added. On *Olympic*'s first, second and third round voyages the receipts totalled £1,730, £1,400 and an estimated £1,250 respectively. Thomas Andrews noted on the ship's maiden voyage that eleven extra four-seat tables were required, but on the third eastbound crossing Cunard's naval architect, Leonard Peskett, noted that 'owing to the great demand for seats in the restaurant the tables have been increased from 25 to 41, thereby providing 33 additional seats.' Cunard were never as keen on the concept and Peskett noted 'the introduction of the restaurant appears to be creating a new class of passenger, who assumes an air of superiority and holds aloof from the ordinary saloon diner.' (George Behe collection)

Top right: In 1911, *The Shipbuilder* published deck plans of *Olympic* and *Titanic*. They represent with reasonable accuracy how *Olympic* appeared when she entered service, but *Titanic*'s design saw a number of changes amidships on B-deck. (*The Shipbuilder*, 1911/Ioannis Georgiou collection)

Centre right: *Titanic*'s B-deck was radically different from how it was originally envisaged: the first-class staterooms were expanded to the ship's side, while the new Café Parisien and enlarged *á la carte* restaurant took up what was originally part of the second-class promenade. (Bruce Beveridge collection)

Bottom right: *Britannic*'s arrangement was an interesting amalgamation of the early *Olympic* and *Titanic*, with the largest *á la carte* restaurant and reception room on board any of the three sister ships, greater luxuries (including private bathroom facilities) and a redesigned starboard side 'parlour suite'. The enclosure of the aft well deck and new location of the third-class smoke room above the poop are also evident. (J. Kent Layton collection)

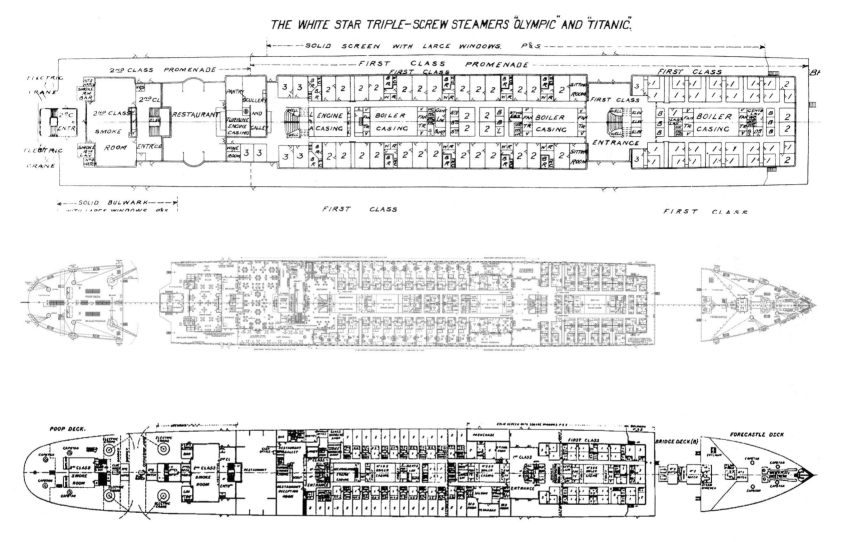

THE WHITE STAR TRIPLE-SCREW STEAMERS "OLYMPIC" AND "TITANIC".

Was it then *Olympic*'s duty to avoid a collision? Captain Smith and the other witnesses from *Olympic* judged that the two ships had been running approximately parallel, which supported the White Star Line's case; but evidence from both ships as to the courses they were on showed that they were converging at an angle of about fifteen degrees. In that case, *Hawke*, on the starboard side, had right of way.

Olympic's senior second engineer, John Herbert Thearle, was asked detailed questions about steam pressure and the ship's speed. Under hostile questioning, he denied that he was trying to 'cut down the speed... as

much as possible'. The wheelhouse clock, which was used by Sixth Officer Holehouse to record the times in the rough deck log, only showed minutes, whereas the ship's master clock, inside the chart room, showed seconds as well. Depending on whether the collision had taken place a few seconds after 12.46 p.m. or a few seconds before 12.47 p.m., the difference between a roughly three- or four-minute interval made a significant difference to the speed *Olympic* had reached.

David Watson Taylor, a naval constructor for the United States, testified as to the sheer force of water displaced by *Olympic*. 'In my opinion, with two

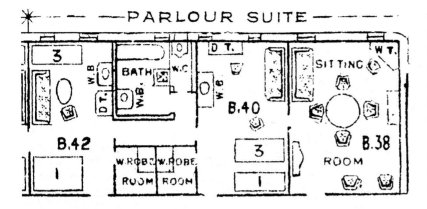

— · — · — PARLOUR SUITE — · — · —

vessels in those relative positions… there would develop strong suction… tending to draw the bow of the *Hawke* towards *Olympic*… After the sheer had once begun it would rapidly become irresistible.' White Star's case that *Hawke*'s helm had been mistakenly starboarded was dealt a blow, even though witnesses such as Captain Pritchard, formerly *Mauretania*'s commander, stated that he had not experienced any suction or interaction between ships in narrow channels during his lengthy career.

Sir Samuel Evans, the presiding judge, concluded that: 'there was no starboarding [turning to port] by the *Hawke* as contended by the *Olympic* – and I am of the opinion that in the exceptional conditions which prevailed, the forces set up in the water are sufficient to account for the *Hawke* being

Above: One of *Olympic*'s four 'parlour suites': the port side suite on B-deck. (*The Shipbuilder*, 1911/Ioannis Georgiou collection)

Right: The sitting room, B38, in Louis XVI style had carved walnut and sycamore panelling. The period staterooms were still admired as among the finest afloat in 1935. (*The Shipbuilder*, 1911/Ioannis Georgiou collection)

Above: The Empire-style stateroom, B40, was fitted in white panelling with subtle detailing in gilt. (*The Shipbuilder*, 1911/Ioannis Georgiou collection)

Above right: The Louis XV room was Harland & Wolff's own 'Bedroom A' design with French-style oak panelling. This photograph depicts a similar stateroom to B42. (Ioannis Georgiou collection)

Below: *Titanic*'s 'parlour suite' on the starboard side of B-deck. (George Behe collection)

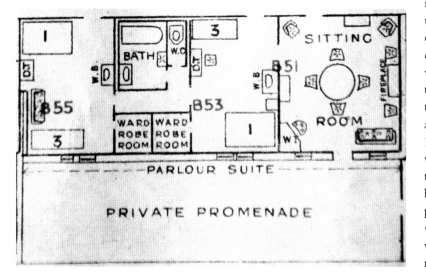

carried towards the *Olympic* in a swerve which was beyond her control.' He ruled they were crossing vessels and *Olympic*'s navigation was at fault. In light of the fact that *Olympic* was under compulsory pilotage at the time of the collision, the White Star Line's defence on that ground succeeded. However, they tried to clear their ship's name and appealed against the verdict. The recovery of *Hawke*'s damaged ram gave them grounds for hope in pinpointing the precise location of the collision, but there was no proof as to precisely when it had fallen off. The original verdict was upheld in April 1913: White Star had not established that '*Hawke* was the overtaking vessel and bound to keep out of the way'; the vessels were crossing and therefore *Olympic* had been required to keep out of *Hawke*'s way; and, as *Hawke* was not to blame for 'what she did or omitted to do' then it followed 'that the cause of the collision was the faulty navigation of the *Olympic*'. Perhaps the company's luck would change. They took their appeal to the House of Lords, then Britain's highest court. By December 1913, it had been discovered that some of the navigating buoys' locations were incorrectly shown on the Admiralty charts in use aboard *Hawke* at the time: since they were shown 60–70 yards further south, then she had been further north and therefore closer to the middle of the channel than previously assumed. That meant that she could have given more room for *Olympic*. However, their mammoth effort was in vain. The final appeal was not dismissed until November 1914, but the company continued to maintain that they were in the right.

One of *Titanic*'s innovations was the addition of a private promenade deck for each of the two B-deck 'parlour suites'. This artist's impression appears to show the one on the port side as originally envisaged, without the wicker furniture or other details as it was completed. In January 1912, the two suites with a private promenade were advertised at $2,250 (winter season); $3,300 (intermediate season) or $4,350 (summer season) for one or two passengers and an accompanying servant. By contrast, even in March 1914 *Olympic*'s B-deck 'parlour suites' – virtually identical save for the promenade – were advertised at $1,000, $1,575 and $2,150 respectively ('$50 extra for each additional passenger'). At the time, £1 was worth about $5. (© National Museums Northern Ireland)

The sitting room, B51, was in Adam style, white panelled throughout with mahogany doors. It was the same style as the counterpart on board *Olympic*, but the fireplace was relocated to the forward bulkhead to make way for a doorway leading to the private promenade. The beautiful bedroom, B53, was in Italian Renaissance, with satinwood panelling and furniture, and the final room, B55, was of 'Bedroom A' design. (*L'Illustration*, 1912/Author's collection, courtesy Daniel Klistorner)

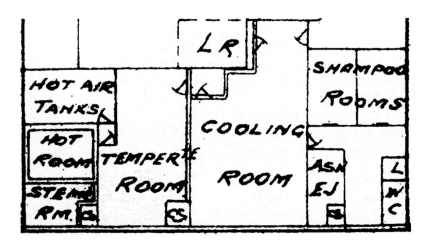

Olympic's Turkish Bath establishment on F-deck. (*The Shipbuilder*, 1911/Ioannis Georgiou collection)

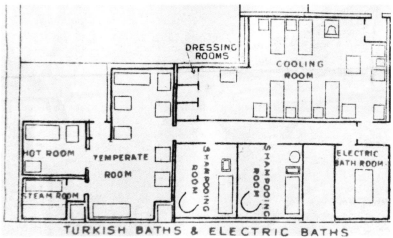

The arrangement of *Titanic*'s Turkish Baths was different to her sister ship's, so that the Cooling Room did not extend to the ship's side. It is also interesting to note the differences between *Olympic*'s baths as depicted on a general arrangement plan to *Titanic*'s as depicted on an accommodation plan for passengers, such as the depiction of the furniture. (George Behe collection)

Left: 'It is doubtful whether the *Olympic* has ever cleared the new dock in such a splendid manner as did the *Titanic* on this occasion,' wrote one observer:

> From the moment she began to move from her berth in that dock she was under absolute control, and she passed out of the dock not only majestically, but also smoothly and calmly. If anything, she was proceeding more slowly than the *Olympic* usually does, and she turned her nose towards the sea with the greatest ease… the tugs seemed to be working magnificently, and once she had turned round and straightened herself for the channel a few of the people standing by began to move homewards, some of them being heard to make exclamations of surprise at the ease with which a 46,000 ton steamer could be shaped for the sea. Indeed, matters were going so well that some of the tugs were able to slacken off. One or two, at least, had left the vessel, and were merely following in her wake until she had cleared the dock head.

As she continued into the channel, she had to pass *Oceanic* and the American liner *New York*, moored alongside, but one by one the lines holding *New York* parted as *Titanic* drew abreast. She began to drift towards *Titanic*, stern first. Quick thinking averted a collision. On *Titanic*'s bridge, the engines were reversed, and the tug *Vulcan* made an important contribution. *New York* was made secure and *Titanic* proceeded. Perhaps her remarkable escape signalled she was destined to be a luckier ship than *Olympic*; others may have thought it a bad start to the maiden voyage. (*L'Illustration*, 1912/Author's collection, courtesy Daniel Klistorner)

Above: A White Star Line advertisement for *Olympic* and *Titanic*'s New York departures in February 1912. Only the first on 21 February 1912 took place as planned: *Olympic* lost a propeller blade three days later and, after returning to Belfast for a new propeller blade, her 16 March and 6 April 1912 departures were changed to 23 March and 13 April respectively. *Titanic*'s 20 April 1912 departure was cancelled after she sank on her maiden voyage. It was reported that over 600 first-class bookings had been made. (Author's collection)

Right: On 7 November 1879, the Guion liner *Arizona* struck an iceberg head on. She survived, but her bow was badly damaged. It is sometimes speculated as to whether *Titanic*, a vessel more than nine times greater in gross tonnage and significantly faster, would have survived a head-on collision. Edward Wilding believed she would have done: 'I am afraid she would have crumpled up in stopping herself. The momentum of the ship would have crushed in the bows for 80 or perhaps 100 feet.' Whether she would have will never be known for sure, but no criticism can be directed reasonably at First Officer William Murdoch for trying to avoid the iceberg entirely. (Author's collection)

No.2 Mrs LEGGETT 2 Relations

No.3 Mrs BULFORD 1 Cousin

No.4 Mr.s WELSH 2 Relations

No.42 Mrs PRESTON Son

No.47 Mrs JAGO, Husband

No.50 Mrs BENSTEAD 2 Cousins

No.51 Mrs WALTON 3 Relations

No.53 Mrs WILTON 1 Cousin

Left: A poignant image: 'Southampton, where the majority of the crew lived, was a city of sorrow as soon as news of the disaster became known.' Milbank Street was one of the 'streets of mourning' and several of the bereaved homes were marked. (*The Deathless Story of the Titanic*, 1912/ Author's collection)

J. Bruce Ismay kept busy. On 1 August 1911, he had written to Cunard's chairman, Alfred Booth, saying that for 'some time' he had been considering a scheme for 'eliminating undue competition' between the leading North Atlantic shipping lines. Perhaps it would involve 'organising a steamship company in which the Cunard, Hamburg-American [HAPAG], North German Lloyd and IMM company would be jointly and equally interested.' The organisation would involve each company's largest liners. Booth was agreeable and HAPAG's Albert Ballin, whose plans for his own trio of enormous liners were well underway, was willing to discuss it.

Press reports that an enlarged sister ship, 1,000ft long and to be called *Gigantic*, had been ordered by White Star led to an exchange of telegrams between Ballin and Ismay. Ballin wrote on 7 December 1911:

Newspapers report you ordered another steamer of the '*Olympic*' type. Referring to a conversation we had at Cologne, think it would be wise policy if we agree not to exceed certain dimensions. Propose 900 by 100 feet. We are discussing contract for a third boat of this type, and shall probably have to order a fourth ship like that within next six months to secure a weekly service from April, 1915. Think it does not pay to continue this race for the largest ship.

Ballin's new vessels were already beyond his proposed length. Ismay responded:

Have seen no newspaper report which gives correct information concerning dimensions [of] our new steamer. Would welcome an understanding amongst leading companies which would restrict competition for owning largest ship… Feel strongly only means [of] preventing unnecessary construction of huge vessels would be some arrangement of joint ownership… We are considering building three additional steamers, in order [to] run semi-weekly service between Southampton and New York.

Ismay wrote on 18 December 1911 that he was pleased at Ballin's willingness to discuss 'an agreement as to the maximum size of ship to be constructed, and an agreement for joint ownership'.

There were other possibilities for mutually beneficial co-operation. On 1 February 1912, Ismay referred Ballin's proposal to Alfred Booth for 'an insurance arrangement calculated to reduce the expenses for insurance by mutual arrangement'. Large ships such as the '*Olympic*' class, *Lusitania* and *Mauretania* were very valuable and insuring them posed difficulties. Booth agreed it could be a good idea, explaining that to avoid 'exorbitant premiums'

Cunard carried 'a larger total loss risk than I at all care about, and I should certainly much prefer to see this risk spread over eight or nine ships rather than concentrated on two or three'.

Following discussions in January and February 1912, Ismay was set to retire as president of IMM on 30 June 1913, when he would be succeeded by Harold Sanderson.[1] He planned to remain as the chairman and managing director of the White Star Line, but in the meantime he had a special family occasion to look forward to, as well as *Titanic*'s maiden voyage. On 10 February 1912, he apologised that he could not meet Ballin on a suggested date: 'my daughter is going to be married on the 21st [March]… we shall have to defer our discussion until some time in May, as it is my intention, all being well, to make the first voyage on the *Titanic* leaving Southampton on the 10th April, being due back about the 27th…'

TITANIC'S MAIDEN VOYAGE

'The workmanship is of the highest class throughout,' wrote Francis Carruthers, ship surveyor to the Board of Trade at Belfast. He had inspected the ship's structure, machinery and equipment throughout construction and was happy with what he saw: the lifeboats were all 'well made and satisfactory'; and 'all the [watertight] doors and frames for the doors were substantial and well made; when completed tests were made of the closing arrangements and the fit after closing of all the doors; all proved satisfactory.' Following her brief trials on 2 April 1912, on the journey down to Southampton *Titanic* 'obtained a speed of about 23.25 knots for several hours' according to Edward Wilding.

Titanic's passenger list included 324 first, 284 second and 709 third class. Her total of 1,317 passengers was almost identical to *Olympic*'s the previous year and still a good showing for April.[2] Contrary to popular belief, it was hardly surprising that she was not full for the maiden voyage. Even the most popular express liners of the period sailed half full on a regular basis. *Mauretania* was in service for three years before she carried more than 2,000 passengers. Older ships such as *Majestic* sailed for years without carrying over 1,000 passengers, even in high season. *Olympic* had already taken out 2,043 passengers the previous week, arriving in New York on the day *Titanic* sailed: 10 April 1912. It would have been a remarkable demand for tickets if they had both sailed that full.

After calling at Cherbourg and Queenstown, *Titanic* departed on schedule and her speed was gradually increased. She logged 484, 519 and 546 miles each day. The ship's second officer, Charles Lightoller, recalled years later: 'Each day, as the voyage went on, everybody's admiration of the ship increased; for the way she behaved, for the total absence of vibration, for her steadiness even with the ever-increasing speed, as she warmed up to her work.' On Saturday afternoon, first-class passenger Elisabeth Lines stopped for coffee in the popular reception room. She did not pay much attention when Captain Smith and J. Bruce Ismay entered and sat nearby, but her curiosity was aroused when she heard them discuss *Titanic*'s performance.

'Well,' Ismay said, 'we did better today than we did yesterday, we made a better run today than we did yesterday, we will make a better run tomorrow.

Left: A detachable pontoon section was one of many fanciful ideas, intended to improve safety at sea, following *Titanic*'s loss. (*Scientific American*, 1912/Author's collection)

THE QUEENSTOWN STOP

★

Even when *Olympic* entered service, the White Star Line already had their doubts about the benefits from calling at Queenstown on the westbound crossing. After leaving Southampton, the express ships called at Cherbourg and then had to deviate towards Queenstown rather than heading straight to New York – a delay that apparently irritated passengers who were eager to get to America. Harold Sanderson believed that the delay averaged out at over seven hours on each crossing. (The Liverpool service did not have the same problems, since the Queenstown call did not entail the same sort of delay for those ships, nor were they as fast as the Southampton vessels.)

By March 1912, just before *Titanic*'s maiden voyage, the company approached the Post Office to discuss omitting the call at Queenstown. As they carried mails, it was necessary to do so and the Post Office was far from keen on the proposal. Following *Titanic*'s loss, the White Star Line did not press the issue, but matters came to a head after *Olympic* returned to service in 1913.

On one occasion when Sanderson was on board *Olympic* at Queenstown, he received a message from Captain Haddock who requested his presence on the bridge. Haddock expressed his concerns about handling a ship of *Olympic*'s enormous size in the relatively confined harbour, telling Sanderson: 'I do not feel at all comfortable about bringing this ship into Queenstown Harbour.'

A rather surprised Sanderson asked 'Why?' and Haddock pointed to the chart in front of them. He felt that the area for safely manoeuvring *Olympic* was too small, and Sanderson reassured him:

Captain Haddock, this is only a temporary matter: you have brought the ship in here safely now a good many times, and I do not want to start any new hare; we are going to end this Queenstown call anyway,

it is only a matter of months now before you are relieved of it, and I would prefer not to approach the Post Office at this moment.

Sanderson cautioned him to 'run no risk that he could possibly be blamed for.'

Olympic had trouble in store when she stopped at Queenstown at 9 a.m. on 25 September 1913. Captain Haddock refused to bring his ship into the inner harbour due to the weather conditions. Attempts to transfer the mails and passengers by tender had to be abandoned at noon. White Star's Liverpool managers wired Captain Haddock at 4 p.m. to say that if the embarkation of passengers could not be completed by that evening, then he would be justified in sailing on to New York. At 6.45 p.m. *Olympic* left behind some amazed passengers at Queenstown: she missed taking on board 213 people – which would have taken her passenger list to almost 2,000 – not to mention 1,500 sacks of mail.

Several prospective first-class passengers voiced their disappointment to the newspapers, and Sanderson had to defend the White Star Line from the inevitable complaints:

It is not the desire or the purpose of the company to discommode passengers or break mail contracts, but in this case we have ample cause. It is conceded that smaller vessels than the *Olympic*, namely, the *Mauretania* and the *Lusitania*, are unsafe in Queenstown Harbour in bad weather. Therefore we do not intend to take any chance of endangering the ship, no matter how many passengers are waiting.

Captain Haddock received no instructions except to clear that dangerous coast before dark and to use his own discretion about embarking passengers. He acted entirely in accord with our wishes, as every sensible person should understand.

Things are working smoothly, the machinery is bearing the test, the boilers are working well.' The two men 'seemed to think a little more pressure could be put on the boilers and the speed increased so that the maiden trip of the *Titanic* would exceed the maiden trip of the *Olympic* in speed.'

'We will beat the *Olympic* and get in to New York on Tuesday,' Ismay remarked. Unencumbered by delays, if *Titanic* simply matched *Olympic*'s speed she would arrive at New York's Ambrose Channel lightship twenty-two minutes after midnight on Wednesday. If she did better then she would pass it on Tuesday evening. The two men headed to the ship's squash court.

By Sunday evening, *Titanic* was approaching the area where ice had been reported. Smith chose not to divert course further south or to slow down. He believed, as did his officers, that any hazard could be seen in time to avoid it. In this, he was no different to other commanders of express liners on the North Atlantic. Passengers settled down for the night, the warm comfort of their staterooms contrasting with the cold outside. First-class passenger Mrs J. Stuart White was about to retire at 11.40 p.m.: 'I was just sitting on the bed, just ready to turn the lights out. It did not seem to me that there was any very great impact at all. It was just as though we went over about a thousand marbles.' A number of passengers realised that something was wrong, whether they felt a tremor or the engines stop. Word soon spread that *Titanic* had collided with an iceberg.

Captain Smith and Purser McElroy were seen heading towards the ship's mail room. Thomas Andrews returned with Smith, telling him: 'Well, three [watertight compartments] have gone already, captain.'[3] Smith ascended towards the bridge, but Andrews continued his inspection. Meanwhile Annie Robinson, one of the first-class stewardesses, had been to the mail room after seeing the two men come back. About half an hour after the collision, she estimated, she saw an alarming sight: 'I saw two mail bags and a man's Gladstone bag, and on looking down the staircase I saw water within six steps of coming on to E-deck.' Mrs Warren, waiting on the D-deck landing, saw Thomas Andrews rushing up the grand staircase: 'He was asked if there was any danger but made no reply. But a passenger who was afterwards saved told me that his face had on it a look of terror. Immediately after this the report became general that water was in the squash courts [sic].' Andrews had discovered the full extent of the flooding and realised it was fatal. *Titanic*'s passengers and crew were in extreme peril. He therefore went up to inform Smith. Andrews estimated initially that she had 'from an hour to an hour and a half'.

After she had been on E-deck, Annie Robinson was told by Andrews: 'Put your lifebelt on and walk about and let the passengers see you.'

'It looks rather mean,' she said.

'No, put it on,' he insisted. 'Well, if you value your life put your belt on.'

★

Titanic sank two hours and forty minutes after the collision, with the loss of 1,496 lives. The Cunard liner *Carpathia*, under Captain Arthur Rostron's command, rescued 712 survivors.[4]

Notes

1   Oldham, *The Ismay Line*, pp.179–83.
2   These figures are based on a name by name analysis by researcher Lester Mitcham.
3   I am grateful to George Behe for sharing his documented analysis of Smith's and Andrews' inspection following the collision.
4   The figure of 712 survivors was obtained from Lester Mitcham's research. It is also based on a name-by-name count.

QUESTIONS OF CONFIDENCE

MUTINY ON THE *OLYMPIC*

John Beaumont, *Olympic*'s chief surgeon, was with Claude Lancaster, the ship's purser, when Robert Fleming, the chief engineer, told them that *Titanic* had been badly damaged in collision with an iceberg and that *Olympic* was heading to assist.[1] It was around midnight, ship's time. All the boilers were called into action and 'the firemen and trimmers down below were straining every nerve to drive the ship'. At maximum speed, *Olympic* 'remained very steady, but vibrated more than usual'; the current was in her favour, but the claim that she made 25 knots was surely exaggerated.[2] Beaumont spent time preparing to receive survivors with his staff, making up 200 beds in the third-class public rooms near the stern. By the time the news came through that *Titanic* had sunk, 'not one' of those on board 'could realise really what had happened'. He knew a number of people on *Titanic*, including Dr O'Loughlin, the chief surgeon, who had told him at Southampton's South Western Hotel that he was tired of changing ships and wanted to stay on *Olympic*. When O'Loughlin told Captain Smith, the commander 'chided him for being lazy, and told him to pack up and come with him'.[3]

A charitable fund received a number of contributions from passengers, but nothing further could be done. *Olympic* dropped passengers at Plymouth and Cherbourg before returning to Southampton on the morning of 21 April 1912. There was further sad news. One of the greasers, A. Galpin, had been taken ill on Thursday 18 April 1912 and transferred to hospital on reaching Southampton, but he died soon afterwards. (On 15 May 1912, Captain Haddock and Dr Beaumont apologised that: 'Owing to the stress of work and worry onboard that particular voyage connected with the *Titanic* disaster the entry… in the log book was inadvertently overlooked.') Despite the 'state of dismay' in Southampton when *Olympic* docked, she had another sailing scheduled. J. Bruce Ismay had instructed that none of the fleet were to leave port without enough lifeboats to accommodate passengers and crew. Sure enough, *Olympic* took on board a number of boats from vessels such as HMT *Soudan*. Captain Clarke, the assistant emigration officer for the Board of Trade who had cleared *Titanic* to sail, reported on 22 April 1912 that there were '40 extra Berthon [collapsible] boats' being fitted. A number were taken off subsequently as they were not required. On Wednesday 24 April 1912, he cleared *Olympic* to sail, but about fifteen minutes before noon a large number of firemen and trimmers left the ship because they were not satisfied with the lifeboat provision. Around 1.30 p.m., Captain Haddock moved his command to an anchorage off Spithead while the White Star Line sought to engage replacements from as far afield as Liverpool and Sheffield.

Clarke reported that he had overseen the lowering of one wooden boat and one Berthon collapsible on sailing day and both were fine. He remained on board and, the next day, two wooden boats and two collapsibles were swung out and two Berthon collapsibles opened up on deck: 'These manoeuvres necessitated lowering and floating the original lifeboats under davits. All was carried out satisfactorily.' One collapsible showed a slow leak, but even so there was 'seating accommodation for two hundred persons in excess of the total expected number of passengers and crew'.

Left: Members of *Olympic*'s stokehold crew, carrying their kits, leave the ship shortly before sailing. (*Illustrated London News*, 1912/Author's collection)

Above: Captain Maurice Harvey Clarke, assistant emigration officer for the Board of Trade at Southampton, inspected *Olympic*'s lifeboats and stated that they were perfectly adequate. He is seen here on the forward starboard boat deck. On the left, smaller vessels illustrate the White Star liner's great size; on the right, the officers' quarters are clearly visible. (*Illustrated London News*, 1912/Author's collection)

Already more than a day late, at 10.30 p.m. a number of replacement firemen and trimmers were brought on board by tender. Another lot followed around midnight. It was hoped that they would be able to make up for some of the time lost by driving the ship at full speed. Unfortunately, there was concern that a number of non-union men were among the replacements and shortly after midnight over fifty seamen left the ship in protest and boarded the tender. Captain Haddock tried to persuade them to return and then even a direct order failed: 'This is mutiny… for the last time I order you [to return].' He requested the assistance of Captain Goodenough, of the naval vessel *Cochrane*. It was 1 a.m. when he came on board to speak to Haddock and the White Star Line's manager at Southampton, Philip Curry. Goodenough recalled:

> I saw the men and asked them what their grievance was. They told me that, in the first place, some of them were not satisfied with the safety of the collapsible boats supplied, but the main question in reality was evidently the quality of the men who were being shipped as firemen from Portsmouth. They all stated that they refused to go to sea in the ship unless they had positive proof that these men were properly qualified firemen, greasers, etc. There were also some remarks about their being non-union men…

He failed to persuade them, even after advising them 'what you are doing now in combining to leave the ship when she is afloat in an open roadstead, as she is now, is an act of open mutiny'. The next morning, 26 April 1912, they were landed ashore and into the custody of the police at Portsmouth. *Olympic*'s voyage was abandoned.

In court, White Star argued that the men had disobeyed the lawful command of Captain Haddock; the defence argued that *Olympic* had been under-manned, and the replacements were 'the scallywags of Portsmouth'. Under cross-examination, *Olympic*'s fifth officer, thirty-year-old John Withers,

Left: A number of crewmen rowing one of the collapsible boats. (*Illustrated London News*, 1912/Author's collection)

Centre left: A 'slight rent' was noted in the side of one of the collapsible boats. (*Illustrated London News*, 1912/Author's collection)

Bottom left: Captain Clarke watches *Olympic*'s crew lower one of the collapsibles before it is opened out. The image gives an idea of what *Titanic*'s passengers would have seen on the night of the disaster, as they came on deck and the lifeboats were readied. (*Illustrated London News*, 1912/Author's collection)

stood his ground and repeatedly used phrases such as 'I don't know', 'I cannot say' or 'I believe so'. He was asked: 'Don't you know there was a consultation at Southampton and there was another long conversation last night?'

'I was in bed,' Withers replied.

'Oh! It didn't interest you very much, then.'

'Well, my watch finished.'

Mr. King, for the defence, found Withers' answers frustrating: 'Don't you wish to answer questions?'

'I am doing my very best.'

'Well, were there not 284 men left at Southampton?'

'You cannot judge numbers,' Withers replied.

'Don't say I cannot judge numbers,' King admonished him. 'I am asking you.'

Mr. Hiscocks, prosecuting on behalf of the White Star Line, stepped in: 'It's quite obvious what he means. When he says "you" he means "I cannot, or anyone else cannot, judge numbers to one or two".'

Second Engineer Charles McKimm testified that the replacement men had been competent for the job. When asked if '"firing" a ship' was 'skilled labour' he responded, 'No, sir, not skilled labour, but hard work,' to much amusement. In the end, the charges were proved but no punishment was handed down. It was not a victory for the seamen: '…the court has found them guilty of an act of wilful disobedience. We have told them their action is wrong in disobeying their captain's order. We came to this decision because we feel there are unusual features in this case which cannot, or which are not likely to occur again.'

Olympic's next sailing would be on 15 May 1912: there were only eighty-eight people in first class out of a total of 527 passengers.

BACK IN SERVICE

On five consecutive westbound crossings, *Olympic* carried fewer than 1,000 passengers, but there were signs of recovery as the weeks went by. In June 1912, she carried 666 first-class passengers from New York; by September 1912, she was bringing 713 first-class passengers to the city. If the White Star Line were pleased that passenger numbers were recovering, *Olympic* experienced her own run of problems throughout the year. According to one account, she avoided a fatal accident seven weeks after *Titanic*'s loss. Near the end of her eleventh eastbound crossing at the start of June 1912, the light began to fade one evening and the officer of the watch was alerted to broken water ahead. Consequently, he had to order the engines reversed to bring the ship to a halt. It transpired that a navigational error had placed her far north of her intended course, so that she had been in danger of grounding off Land's End. Captain Haddock, a public figure who bore ultimate responsibility for *Olympic*'s navigation, was not dismissed, but if the account is to be believed then a close eye was kept on his performance and it appears that he won back the company's confidence over time.[4]

In July 1912, *Olympic* grounded briefly on a mud bank as she was leaving New York. Early the following month, the starboard propeller lost a blade shortly after she left Queenstown, which necessitated a return to Belfast for repairs. Once she was back in service, another blade fell off the port propeller as she approached Plymouth. She completed another round trip at reduced speed. During the crossing, an unfortunate rumour spread that *Olympic* had foundered. It prompted numerous people concerned about their relatives to make enquiries at the White Star Line's offices in Southampton. While groundless, the rumour was all too believable to the public. The White Star Line brought forward her annual overhaul and their plan for an extensive refit.

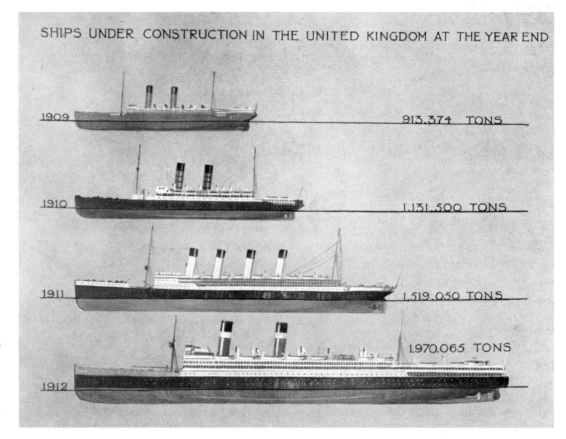

SHIPS UNDER CONSTRUCTION IN THE UNITED KINGDOM AT THE YEAR END

1909 — 913,374 TONS
1910 — 1,131,500 TONS
1911 — 1,519,050 TONS
1912 — 1,970,065 TONS

Right: 'The Shipbuilding Record of 1912'. A diagram showing 'the increase in tonnage of merchant ships building in this country [the United Kingdom] at the end of 1912 over the three previous years. The 542 ships under construction with a tonnage of 1,970,065 is larger than at any other previous period recorded by Lloyd's Register of Shipping… This country builds more ships than all the other countries of the world added together.' At the end of 1912, ships totalling 1,368,671 tons were under construction abroad. (*The Sphere*, 1913 /Author's collection)

An artist's design proposal for the Café Parisien dated 30 October 1912. (National Maritime Museum, Greenwich, London, United Kingdom G10679)

Below: *Olympic* carried over 1,500 passengers to New York, where she arrived on 9 April 1913. (*Illustrated London News*, 1913/Author's collection)

One passenger who had enjoyed crossing on *Olympic* was an American lady in her mid-forties, Bertha M. Colburn. She returned to America after enjoying seeing the sights in Britain during the summer. Bertha made sure all her luggage was in her stateroom and then watched the 'great cranes swing the trunks onboard'. *Olympic* was an hour late in departing, and it was 'slowly, slowly down the river,' she remembered. The Channel crossing was smooth and they reached Cherbourg around 7 p.m. Even after the two tenders, *Nomadic* and *Traffic*, had unloaded their passengers and luggage, she wrote that 'this boat [sic] is so immense that there is more than room to spare.' She was particularly impressed with *Olympic*'s size and steadiness. On the promenade deck, she noted it was: 'Open and has space for five or six persons to walk abreast, beyond the rows of deckchairs – which however are not yet even half-filled, perhaps because it is so comfortable withindoors…' As the voyage went on, she noted: 'no one seems to be seasick. The boat moves

The White Star Line were keen to show prospective passengers what *Olympic* offered. The photo of the first-class reading and writing room depicts its appearance after the 1912–13 refit: the original small alcove has been closed off to make way for additional first-class staterooms, so that the original L-shaped room is now a rectangular shape. In a brochure published after the war, the company used a picture from 1911 that showed an alcove which no longer existed. (Author's collection)

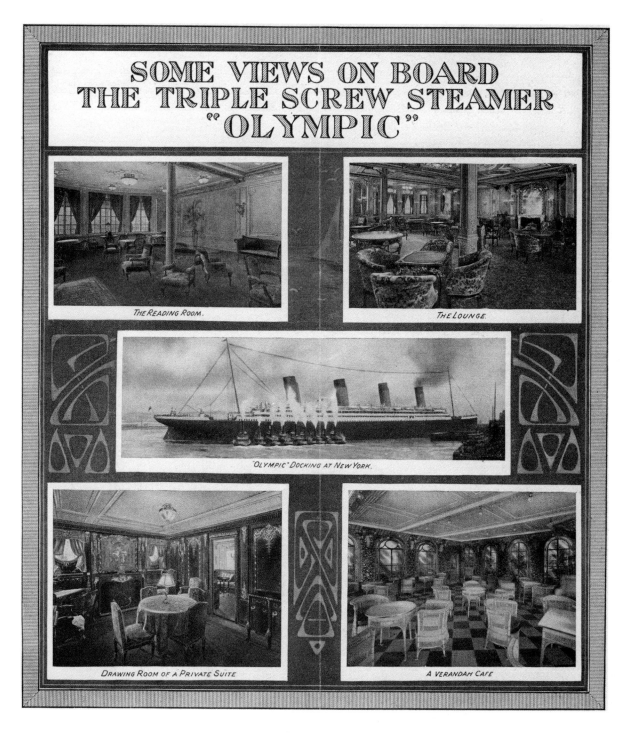

SOME VIEWS ON BOARD THE TRIPLE SCREW STEAMER "OLYMPIC"

THE READING ROOM.

THE LOUNGE.

"OLYMPIC" DOCKING AT NEW YORK.

DRAWING ROOM OF A PRIVATE SUITE

A VERANDAH CAFE

★

he watertight subdivision of *Olympic* and *Titanic* incorporated a number of improvements compared to earlier ships built by Harland & Wolff. The double bottom, itself deep enough to walk through, was subdivided into numerous compartments and was unusual in that it was extended up to the turn of the bilge (where the ship's bottom met the sides). This gave additional protection if the ship grounded with a list. Fifteen watertight bulkheads divided the hull into sixteen main watertight compartments. The watertight bulkhead plating was from 10 to 20 per cent in excess of Lloyd's requirements, while the stiffening was 75 to 100 per cent greater. In the event that the two largest watertight compartments were completely flooded, they would remain afloat with a margin of safety. In fact, under many scenarios they would have remained afloat with three compartments flooded, and even the first four compartments from the bow.

Since access was required for the working of the ship, the design of the watertight doors was important: the heavy cast-iron doors dividing the machinery spaces slid in heavy cast-iron frames. They could be closed electrically from the bridge; from the deck above the top of the watertight bulkhead; by hand next to the door; or by a float beneath that

would rise up if flooding occurred. 'The doors were arranged to drop and close in 30 seconds from the time the electric contact was made from the bridge or when pulling the handle near the door.' Once they had been closed from the bridge, they could not be opened again without the officer's permission, which was a new feature introduced for the first time on *Olympic*. In addition to the main doors throughout the boiler and machinery compartments, there were a number of others on the higher decks which were manually operated. The pumps were 'unusually elaborate, and so arranged that any compartment which was flooded could be isolated, together with any valve in it left open; and no matter what pair of compartments in the machinery space might be flooded, pumps could still be applied to any compartment in the ship.'

Although they did not follow the model of *Lusitania* and *Mauretania*, which were built to Admiralty specification, there were good reasons for Harland & Wolff to avoid the use of watertight decks (which could cause a loss of stability if flooding occurred above them) and longitudinal watertight bulkheads (which could cause a severe list if flooding occurred along the ship's side compartments). Naval architects disagreed on the subject at the time, for there were advantages and disadvantages to each model depending on the circumstances.

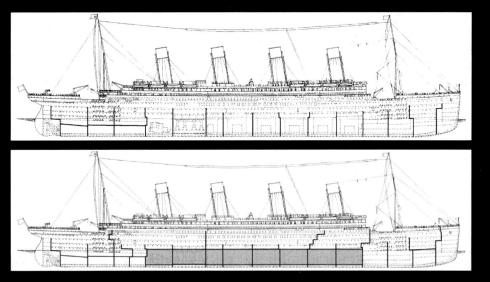

Olympic's watertight subdivision as she was originally built in 1911, the same configuration as *Titanic*.

Olympic's watertight subdivision following the 1913 refit, which was essentially the same for *Britannic*. The inner skin is shaded in grey. (Author's collection, illustrations by Bruce Beveridge)

The White Star liners *Teutonic* and *Majestic* were originally built with longitudinal bulkheads, which were subsequently removed by Harland & Wolff as they came to consider them dangerous.) Harland & Wolff's original design compares favourably with modern ships' watertight subdivision.

Olympic saw many changes in 1913. 'After the accident to the *Titanic*, certain alterations were decided on, with a view to increasing the margin of safety. We had arranged prior to that,' Edward Wilding explained, 'for any two compartments flooded. The owners desired, in view of the character of the accident, to see that she would float with a large number of compartments flooded.' Five of the watertight bulkheads were extended to B-deck and the stiffening correspondingly increased for their greater height; a new watertight bulkhead was installed, dividing the electric engine room; a new watertight deck was fitted in the first forward hold; improvements were made to the hatches; and an inner skin was fitted extending the length of the boiler and machinery compartments. (While designing it, the shipbuilder bore in mind the possibility that she would be converted to oil fuel in future, and so they incorporated features into the inner skin so that it could be used for the purpose.) Several bulkheads which originally extended watertight to D-deck were effectively reduced in height so that they extended watertight to E-deck. Wilding believed that a single new watertight deck was acceptable in the one hold. Following her maiden voyage, *Olympic*'s Chief Engineer Joseph Bell recommended the installation of an indicator on the bridge showing whether the watertight doors were closed or not, and this feature was installed on *Olympic* and *Britannic*.

As a result of the modifications, *Olympic* could float with several different groups of six watertight compartments flooded, or even seven compartments from the stern, providing the portholes were closed; with the forward six compartments completely flooded, the forepeak would be submerged and the foredecks awash, but she would remain afloat.

Above: 'The New *Olympic*' as the White Star Line advertised her in *Harper's Magazine* for the 1913 season. (Author's collection)

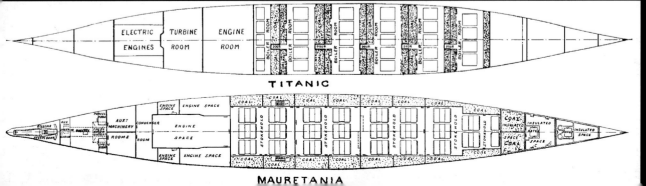

Left: In May 1912, the *Scientific American* compared *Titanic*'s watertight subdivision to that of *Mauretania*. (*Scientific American*, 1912/ Author's collection)

FIRST CLASS RATES S. S. "OLYMPIC"

From New York to Plymouth, Cherbourg or Southampton / From Southampton or Cherbourg to New York	Winter Season 16th Aug. to 31st March / 1st Nov. to 31st March			Intermediate Season 1st to 30th April 1st to 15th August / 1st April to 31st July 16th to 31st Oct.			Summer Season 1st May to 31st July / 1st Aug. to 15th Oct.		
	For 3	For 2	For 1	For 3	For 2	For 1	For 3	For 2	For 1
BOAT DECK OUTSIDE ROOM—									
Z	....	$300	$250	....	$400	$350	....	$500	$450
OUTSIDE SINGLE BERTH ROOMS—									
T, U, W	....	....	150	....	....	235	....	...	325
Y	....	....	150	....	....	225	....	....	300
UPPER PROMENADE DECK "A" OUTSIDE ROOMS—									
A 37, 46 with Private Bath and Toilet	$450	400	350	$650	600	550	850	800	750
A 38, 40 with Private Bath and Toilet	....	400	350	....	600	550	....	800	750
A 3, 4	420	350	300	540	470	425	$675	600	550
A 34, 35	405	350	300	495	450	400	600	550	500
A 36	....	350	300	....	450	400	....	550	500
SINGLE BERTH ROOMS—									
▲Outside, A 11, 12, 16, 17, 20, 21, 24, 25, 28, 29, 32, 33, 44	....	....	175	....	....	260	....	....	350
Outside, A 1, 2, 7, 8	....	...	150	....	....	225	....	....	300
●Inside, A 5, 6, 9, 10, 14, 15, 18, 19, 22, 23, 26, 27, 30, 31	....	....	M	....	....	190	....	....	250
Inside, A 42	....	....	M	....	....	165	....	....	200
		For 2 each			For 2 each			For 2 each	
▲Rooms A 11, 12, 16, 17, 20, 21, 24, 25, 28, 29, 32, 33 are so fitted that a Sofa Berth for a second passenger can be provided when required at the following rates per berth	....	$135	....	....	$165	....	....	$200	....
Rooms A 7, 8	....	M	....	....	155	....	....	180	....
●These rooms are so fitted that a Sofa Berth for a second passenger can be provided when required at the following rates per berth	....	M	....	....	$140	....	....	$150	....
PROMENADE DECK "B" OUTSIDE ROOMS—PARLOR SUITES—									
✠B 40, 42, 44 / B 37, 39 41 { Comprising two Bedrooms, Drawing Room, Private Bath and Toilet. Each Bedroom is fitted with a Wardrobe Room	One or Two Passengers $1,000 ($50 extra for each additional passenger)			One or Two Passengers $1,575 ($50 extra for each additional passenger)			One or Two Passengers $2,150 ($50 extra for each additional passenger)		
	For 3	For 2	For 1	For 3	For 2	For 1	For 3	For 2	For 1
✠B 43, 45, 46, 48, 49, 51, 52, 54, 55, 57, 58, 60, with Private Bath and Toilet. Each Room is fitted with a Wardrobe Room	....	$450	$400	....	$725	$675	....	$1,000	$950
✠B 63, 66, with Private Bath and Toilet	....	400	350	....	625	575	....	850	800
✠B 65, with Private Bath and Toilet	$450	400	350	$650	600	550	$850	800	750
	For 3 each	For 2 each	For 1	For 3 each	For 2 each	For 1	For 3 each	For 2 each	For 1
✠B 43, 45, 46, 48, 49, 51, 52, 54, 55, 57, 58, 60, each Room is fitted with Wardrobe Room	....	$175	$300	....	$250	$450	....	$325	$600
✠B 47, 50, 53, 56, 59, 61, 62, 64	....	175	300	....	235	425	....	300	550
B 35, 36, 67	$135	150	250	$165	210	375	$200	275	500
B 11	140	175	300	170	225	400	200	275	500
B 1, 2, 5, 6	....	135	175	....	180	285	....	225	400
Inside Rooms B 68, 69, 70, 71	M	M	150	135	155	225	140	180	300
OUTSIDE ROOMS, SINGLE BERTH—									
■B 7, 8, 9, 10, 12, 14, 15, 16, 17, 18, 19, 20, 21, 22, 23, 24, 25, 26, 27, 28, B 29, 30, 31, 32, 33, 34	....	....	175	....	....	260	....	....	350
B 3, 4	....	....	150	....	....	225	....	....	300
INSIDE ROOM—									
B 38	....	....	M	....	....	165	....	....	200
■Rooms B 7, 8, 9, 10, 12, 14, 15, 16, 17, 18, 19, 20, 21, 22, 23, 24, 25, 26, 27, 28, 29, 30, 31, 32, 33 and 34 are so fitted that a Lower Sofa Berth for a second passenger can be provided, when required, at the following rates per berth	....	$135	....	....	$165	....	....	$200	....

(Continued on next two pages)   ✠ No Single Berths will be let in these rooms
For conditions governing rebates in connection with the a la Carte Restaurant see page 2
THE RIGHT is reserved to alter rates without notice

Right: An advertisement for *Olympic*'s *á la carte* restaurant the same month. On the eastbound leg of her maiden voyage, as first-class bookings mounted there was concern that they would not all fit in the main saloon. The White Star Line introduced a rebate of $25 from the ticket price if a first-class passenger agreed to eat in the restaurant during the voyage. Leonard Peskett felt that 'the restaurant certainly finds a place for that class of passenger who is always dissatisfied with the catering on every ship in which he may travel…The question, however, is whether, after having to pay a restaurant account for one voyage, he will not be more content to take, without demur, his food in the saloon. The rebate from passage money for taking meals in the restaurant is stated to be £5 [$25]. Judging from reports, this amount would scarcely suffice for one day's patronage.' (For a dinner party of three or more people, the minimum rate per head was 12s 6d in August 1911.) (Author's collection)

Far right: The company were proud of their new *Britannic*. Her gross tonnage would exceed *Olympic*'s and make her the largest British vessel afloat. (Author's collection)

Above: 'First Class Rates SS *Olympic*', March 1914. It is interesting that A-deck was referred to as the 'upper promenade' deck and B-deck as the 'promenade'; the official nomenclature was the promenade deck (A) and bridge deck (B). The luxurious 'parlour' and other suites on liners of *Olympic*'s ilk were 'necessary not only because in summer time many persons are willing to pay the price, but also because they form a means for the line to be extra nice to favoured persons when the suites are not booked', according to one shipping official quoted by the *New York Times* in September 1913. Rates dropped to $140 for an inside stateroom on E-deck during the winter season. (Author's collection)

Right and far right: Companies often sought to advertise the fact that their products were being used on board some of the most prestigious vessels afloat. These included the Brown Brothers & Co. steering telemotor and Sirocco fans supplied by Davidson & Co. Ltd. (*Shipbuilding and Shipping Record*, 1914/ Author's collection)

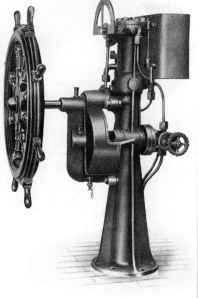

Right: The first-class smoke rooms on *Olympic* and *Titanic* bore substantial similarities to earlier White Star liners. There were subtle differences in that *Olympic*'s was tiled in grey and buff and *Titanic*'s in red and blue, leading to speculation that the green leather seen on chairs on board *Olympic* may have been changed to a red leather on *Titanic*. However, an artist's impression of *Britannic*'s smoke room shows a completely fresh design. The central dome envisaged in early 'Olympic' class design concepts was restored; a new accumulator room meant that the smoke room was an 'L' rather than a 'U' shape; the bay windows became rectangular; and the entire decorative scheme was reconsidered so that the room would be panelled in cedar of Lebanon, reportedly inspired by an apartment at Hampton Court. (© National Museums Northern Ireland)

Below: *Britannic*'s first-class forward grand staircase, seen in an artist's impression of how it would appear when completed. The door at the foot of the stairs accessed the organ, a new and impressive feature not present on *Olympic* or *Titanic*. (© National Museums Northern Ireland)

Above: *Britannic* was unique among her sister ships in the way her lifeboats were handled. The design following the *Titanic* disaster envisaged eight enormous 'girder'-type sets of davits, so that each davit station held a large number of boats. The electrically driven davits ensured that 'a very large number of boats can, one after the other, be put over the side of the vessel and lowered to the waterline in much less time than was possible under the old system of davits.' White Star noted that 'one of the advantages of the new system is that the passengers take their places in the boats expeditiously and with perfect safety before the boats are lifted from the deck of the vessel, and the gear is so constructed that the fully laden boats are lowered at a very considerable distance from the side of the ship, thus minimising risk in bad weather. Moreover, the whole of the boats on board can be lowered on either side of the vessel, whichever happens to be clear, and the gear has been kept so far inboard as to give a wide passage at either side of the ship for promenading, and for marshalling the passengers in case of emergency.' In reality, the position of the funnels prohibited moving them to the other side at several of the boat stations.

Harland & Wolff and William Edward Armstrong, 'all of Queen's Island shipbuilding and engineering works, Belfast', filed a number of applications for patents for the davits, starting in November 1912 and running through to full approval in March 1914. When *Britannic* was launched, it was reported she would carry forty-eight lifeboats: forty-four boats, at 34ft long the largest yet fitted on a ship; two smaller 'cutters' and two motorboats, reportedly built by Maynard on subcontract from John Thornycroft & Co. (Thornycroft Yard Nos 766 and 767). The motorboats were 34ft long, larger than equivalents on board *Aquitania*, while they were capable of forty hours' cruising with their 15 horsepower engines. Passenger capacities were given as between twenty and thirty. (Ioannis Georgiou collection)

Below: *Britannic*'s swimming pool was a marked improvement compared to *Olympic*'s. By 1913, the German liner *Imperator* was in service and sported a larger swimming pool complete with Roman décor and Pompeian columns. The bare metalwork of *Britannic*'s hull, piping and other fixtures were concealed behind panels. It is interesting to note that *Olympic*'s pool remained essentially unchanged throughout a number of refits until the end of her life. (© National Museums Northern Ireland)

so steadily that often one would not know we were in motion. Yesterday they said there was a heavy swell, but we never knew it.' *Olympic*'s interiors impressed her:

> The reading and writing rooms are big and *light* [original emphasis] and airy: the lounge where men may smoke is big and comfortable; just outside the dining room is another big lounge where men may smoke, and take after dinner coffee, and where there is music each evening by a good orchestra; around each stairway is also a large room with easy chairs, the top one being a music room: above is also a gymnasium, and below Turkish Baths, swimming pool, etc., etc. Elevators, three in number, run all the time. The dining room is immense, but divided by alcoves, and the windows are of stained glass. In fact [the] portholes are covered, and everywhere one seems in a big luxurious hotel.

Her one complaint was that 'the cooking is, however, too English – too un-spiced.' The day before reaching New York, she recorded:

> We have had pleasant weather ever since we started, and fairly smooth seas, although there has been some swell at times, and yesterday morning we were surprised to find little racks on the tables, under the cloths. Today however the sea has been like glass – most uninteresting, and as the Englishwoman whom we met at Stratford remarked about any drinking hot water instead of tea: 'how very dull!'

Usually *Olympic* would have arrived early on Wednesday morning, but on this voyage she did not reach the Ambrose Channel until Thursday morning.

Neither Bertha, nor any other impressed travellers would have the option to take *Olympic* over the following winter. She arrived at Belfast on 10 October 1912 for an extensive refit and did not leave until 22 March 1913. As well as changes to her watertight subdivision, she saw other improvements that had been applied to *Titanic*, including additional first-class staterooms on the boat deck in an extended officers' quarters; the *á la carte* restaurant was expanded, with a new reception room, alongside a new Café Parisien; and the popular first-class reception room was enlarged by reducing the entrance halls on either side of the staircase.

It was clear that her popularity was being restored. On two occasions *Olympic* carried more than 700 first-class passengers, including the 752 first-class passengers that she brought to New York in September 1913. Her list included 509 second and 1,003 third class. 'Waterloo Station was jammed this morning when the boat train departed in three long sections,' one newspaper explained. That year, she carried almost 32,000 passengers at an average of 1,325 per crossing and in 1914 she welcomed her 100,000th passenger. The White Star Line's profits rose to a new record in 1913, but their competitors had not gone away.

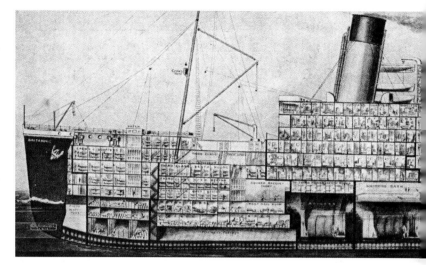

MEETING THE COMPETITION

Olympic's performance was so satisfactory that Ismay's mind was made up. On 28 June 1911, as she left New York for the first time, Harland & Wolff instructed the shipyard and engine works to proceed with the order for 'Yard Number 433'. The third sister ship would be improved all round by the lessons learned from *Olympic* and *Titanic*'s service, setting even higher standards of accommodation. The White Star Line knew that Cunard's *Aquitania* would be in service by 1914, while the plans for HAPAG's *Imperator*, *Vaterland* and *Bismarck* were even further advanced.

Despite exaggerations in the press, the new ship would be very similar to her older sisters. She was the same length, although her breadth was increased by 18in and her keel was laid on 30 November 1911. Consequently, her gross tonnage and displacement would be greater, while a desire to maintain the same speed as her sisters with plenty of power in reserve led to an increase in engine power and a number of refinements to her propelling machinery. Her twenty-four double-ended boilers were increased in length by 1ft; the reciprocating engines saw several refinements and their power was increased; and the low-pressure turbine correspondingly enlarged. She would be capable of maintaining 21 knots with ample power in reserve. The structural design included alterations due to her greater breadth and a number of refinements based on experience. Harland & Wolff made no radical departure from tried-and-tested practice.

The most significant changes stemmed from the *Titanic* disaster: the improved watertight subdivision and inner skin as incorporated into *Olympic* and the arrangements of the ship's lifeboat apparatus, which were a dramatic change. The provision of eight sets of giant 'girder'-type davits, which held a number of lifeboats each, required structural reinforcement due to the concentration of weight at each boat station. Part of the first-class smoke room was sacrificed to make way for a new accumulator room, which was available for the ship's emergency circuit. A pneumatic tube aided communication between the bridge and the Marconi wireless room, while information about the bridge instruments prompted comment on 'the complete control which the captain exercises from the navigating bridge'.

Britannic's passenger accommodation was very similar to *Olympic* and *Titanic*'s, combining their best features with numerous improvements. Many of them had probably been decided on before the disaster. A new children's playroom was included opposite the gymnasium on the boat deck; the forward end of A-deck was enclosed with similar windows to *Titanic*'s; on B-deck the *á la carte* restaurant was expanded and a new reception room added resulting in the removal of the Café Parisien; a new ladies barber's shop and manicurist were added alongside the gents barber's shop; the port side 'parlour suite' retained its promenade, while the starboard suite was allocated its own veranda; and a promenade was retained forward of the grand staircase. The attention to detail can be seen in some of the specifications for the starboard side 'parlour suite': 'The saloon to have round table in the centre constructed as to extend for the accommodation of four persons; four chairs

to be supplied for the dining table; a sofa bed; four arm chairs; a corner writing table and chairs, a small square table and chair; a sideboard and fireplace'; 'the servants' rooms to be finished in dark mahogany and fitted with bed having Pullman [upper berth] over, sofa, wardrobe, folding lavatory, electric heater and a red carpet…' On C-deck another two sitting rooms were included that were fitted permanently as sitting rooms, in addition to those in the four 'parlour' suites. The three elevators serving the grand staircase now continued to the boat deck and a fourth elevator was added further aft running from B-deck to E-deck.

One of the most important improvements could easily be overlooked: private bathroom facilities. In 1911 *Olympic* had a total of forty-two private bathrooms in first class; one set of *Britannic's* general arrangement plans showed 107 private bathrooms with toilets, 39 bathrooms without a toilet and 55 toilets, or a total of 201 assorted private bathroom facilities. Several on E-deck served interchangeable first- and second-class staterooms. Another feature was the improved plumbing system, so that hot water was available immediately rather than having to wait for cold water to warm up. *The Shipbuilder* noted that every first-class stateroom had its own electric fan, while improvements were made to the ventilation system.

Second-class passengers had a new feature with their own gymnasium and an additional enclosed promenade. Changes in third class included the relocation of the ship's hospital and consequent removal of the smoke room to a new deckhouse above the poop deck. New entrances provided access to the fore well deck at the bow and a number of new staircases throughout

An interesting cutaway profile of *Britannic* in two halves, drawn by George Morrell and showing the ship's passenger, crew and machinery spaces. (*The Graphic*, 1916/Author's collection)

helped third-class passengers access the higher decks. These changes may have stemmed from changing Board of Trade regulations. (In July 1911, surveyors were notified of a new rule that would be interpreted to mean: 'stairways from emigrants' quarters on any of the [lower] decks, are to be led up to the open air immediately above the compartment from which the stairs are fitted'. Cunard did not like it and sought White Star's support in requesting an amendment. Their information was forwarded to Lord Pirrie in January 1912.) Numerous improvements, down to the smallest details, were made for *Britannic*: the Litosilo deck coverings used on *Olympic* and *Titanic* were changed to Veitchi.

In May 1912, the *New York Times* reported optimistically that work on the new ship would be accelerated, but 'it will be over a year before the new ship will be completed'. By August 1912, Phillip Franklin, IMM's vice president, indicated that she was expected to enter service early in 1914: even faster than *Olympic* had been built. When IMM's annual report for 1912 was published on 2 June 1913, it was the first to refer to her by her name and explained that *Britannic* would 'be launched early next year'. Work progressed steadily: by 20 September 1913 the hull was fully plated and the launch date was set for 26 February 1914. Following its success, *Britannic* was moved to

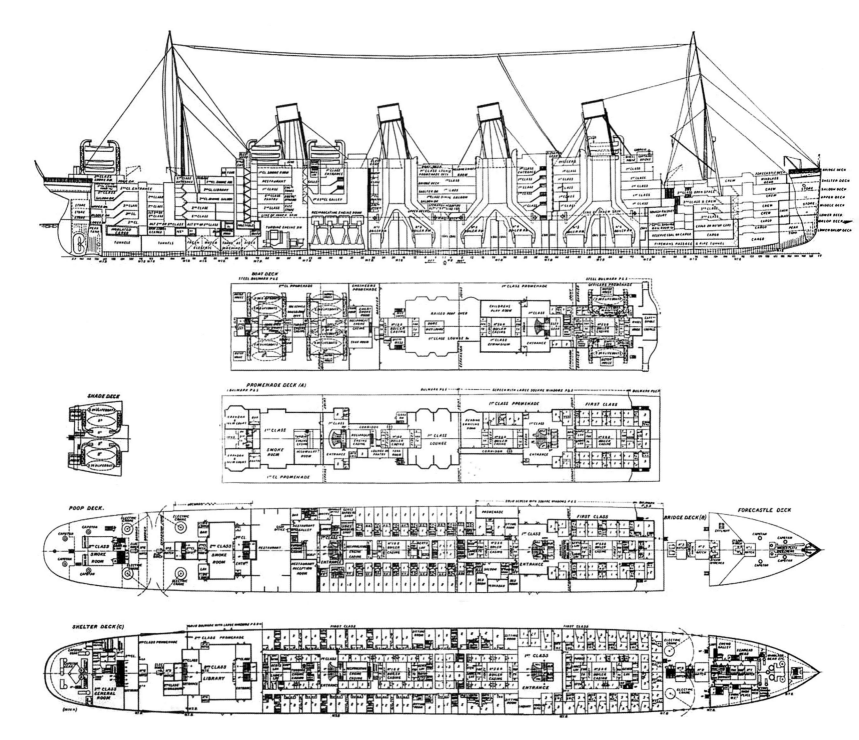

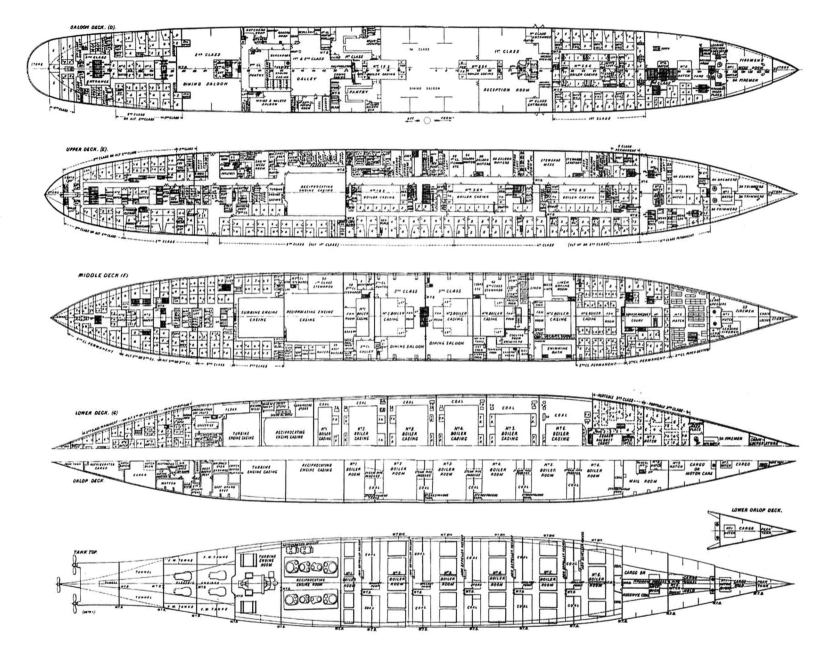

Britannic's deck plans help to understand the ship's layout. It is interesting to note a number of features unique to *Britannic*, such as the children's playroom on the port side of the boat deck opposite the gymnasium; the new first-class staterooms between the reading and writing room and the first-class grand staircase (added to *Olympic* in 1912–13); the accumulator room and redesigned first-class smoke room layout; the shade deck, aft; the third-class smoke room, now aft on B-deck with its original location below used for the ship's hospital. (J. Kent Layton collection)

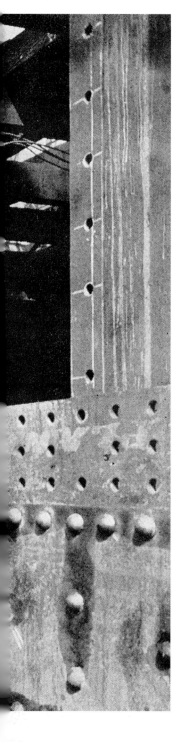

Left: Hydraulic riveting of *Britannic*'s topside shell plating in May 1913. (Mark Chirnside/Ioannis Georgiou/ Daniel Klistorner collection)

Above: *Britannic*'s hull was fully plated by 20 September 1913. This image was published by *Leslie's Weekly* in March 1914. It is interesting that the publication referred to the watertight compartments being 'intended to make the new giant unsinkable' without any qualification. (*Leslie's Weekly*, 1914/Author's collection)

Left: *Britannic*, pictured in an imaginary scene at sea with the White Star Line's first ship of the name. The image was intended to demonstrate the progress of shipbuilding: the new vessel was described as 'a twentieth century ship in every sense of the word'. The comparative theme also appeared in a postcard of the two ships' builders models, contrasting '*Britannic*, 5,000 tons, built in 1874' and '*Britannic*, 50,000 tons, built in 1914'. The earlier ship made her maiden voyage from Liverpool in June 1874, completing 271 round trips during her service life, steaming 2,232,999 miles and carrying 112,711 first- and 282,685 third-class passengers. Hopes were high that the new vessel would do even better. (© Bettmann/Corbis)

Below: *Britannic*'s turbine rotor. Unlike the turbine engines for *Olympic* and *Titanic*, which were sub-contracted to John Brown & Co., *Britannic*'s turbine was built by Harland & Wolff. It received exhaust steam from the reciprocating engines at an increased pressure of 10 pounds per square inch and developed 18,000 shaft horsepower while running at about 170 revolutions. Its weight increased from 420 to 490 tons, making it the heaviest afloat. It was physically the largest ever constructed for marine use, but not the most powerful. (Ioannis Georgiou collection)

Right: *Britannic*'s reciprocating engines were the largest triple expansion marine reciprocating engines ever constructed. They were assembled in the engine works, as with other propelling machinery, then lowered into the ship, reassembled and installed after launch. (Mark Chirnside/ Ioannis Georgiou/Daniel Klistorner collection)

Olympic, as she looked in 1911, has been altered to represent her sister *Britannic*. The advent of larger German ships may explain the White Star Line's reticence to release the new ship's precise dimensions, referring to her as 'about 900 feet long'. To this day, her overall length is sometimes given as 903ft, which possibly originates from a news report that stated she would be 20ft longer than her sisters. Even in 1915, Edward Wilding was unwilling to divulge the precise dimensions. (Author's collection)

the outfitting wharf, where her propelling machinery would be installed and the magnificent interiors would become a reality. She was expected to enter service early in 1915.[5]

The largest British ship was described as 'the highest achievement of her day in the practice of shipbuilding and marine engineering'. Her passenger capacities were given as 790 first, 836 second and 953 third class. While outfitting work continued, *Olympic* and *Oceanic* maintained the express service from Southampton; *Vaterland* and *Aquitania* entered service in May 1914; and the White Star Line looked forward to *Britannic*'s completion. Their plans were shattered when war broke out at the start of August 1914.

Notes

1   Beaumont, John C.H., *Ships and People* (Geoffrey Bles: 1926), pp.97–98.

2   Harold Sanderson cited company records which showed that *Olympic* had maintained 24.2 knots over a twenty-four-hour period on the North Atlantic. However, the date or occasion were not specified.

3   Beaumont, *Op. cit.*, p.100.

4   Weaver, Maurice and Steel, Edwin with Brian Ticehurst, '*Titanic's* Sister Ship Headed for the Rocks', *Titanic Commutator*, 1988, vol.XII, pp.40–41.

5   IMM's annual report for 1913, published on 15 June 1914.

Britannic's launch on Thursday 26 February 1914 was a success, although the weather was not perfect. The event was filmed for posterity and a number of rare still images from the film show the ship's progress: 'The crack of a rocket, and all men beneath the vessel stand clear, the numerous lamps beneath her, by whose light the men had worked, cease to glow, and then – the crack of a second rocket, and the *Britannic* slowly begins to move towards the element that is to be her home.' As she did, Harland & Wolff workers on board, gathered at the forward end of the A-deck promenade and on the port wing of the bridge, waved to those below (above left); picking up speed, the ship's stern entered the water (above right); and the entire vessel was soon afloat, her mighty side towering over spectators (below left). From the time the button was pressed to the time she was afloat, eighty-one seconds elapsed, the hull reaching a maximum speed of 9.5 knots.

Like her sister ships, it was not until outfitting was well advanced that she was dry-docked to have her propellers fitted. *Britannic*'s port and starboard propellers were essentially the same as *Titanic*'s, although their diameter was increased by 3in to 23ft 9in. Her centre propeller was identical to that fitted to *Olympic* when she entered service in 1911. Here, the rapidly rising water is being let into the dry dock before *Britannic* can be floated out (below right). (Footage supplied by British Pathé)

SISTERS AT WAR

Captain Haddock halted the usual wireless reports, ordering portholes covered and the dimming of *Olympic*'s lights. The ship's speed was increased and she reached Quarantine on Tuesday evening. Passengers would disembark at the dock in New York the following morning, 5 August 1914. Disruption at Southampton meant that she returned to Liverpool, without passengers. The White Star Line organised a temporary service as passengers rushed back to America. When *Olympic* arrived in New York on 29 August 1914 she had 810 first- and 646 second-class passengers crammed in, with only 306 in third class. Beaumont recalled: 'We were crowded out with hundreds of Americans who had fled from the continent on the declaration of war, and were thankful to be on board, for bodily they were tired out, mentally annoyed and worried, their baggage mostly lost, stolen, or strayed, and with American money, which was good, but for which English gold could not be obtained.' *Olympic* made another sailing from Liverpool in September, but she returned to Glasgow. One final round trip was then scheduled from Glasgow to New York.

HMT *OLYMPIC*

One of the most dramatic events of *Olympic*'s war years came before her civilian service came to a close. When she left New York on 21 October 1914, her passenger accommodation was deserted: only thirty-five first class,

fourteen second class and 106 third-class passengers. White Star planned to have her laid up once the crossing was completed, but any hopes of an uneventful voyage were discarded when the Marconi apparatus picked up a distress call as *Olympic* rounded the north of Ireland.

Captain Dampier noticed a 'dull noise aft' shortly before 9 a.m. on 27 October 1914. His command, HMS *Audacious*, was on manoeuvres and he wondered if one of the ship's guns had been fired accidentally. In fact, it was soon obvious that the ship had been badly damaged by an explosion: he suspected a torpedo. Although he ordered the watertight doors closed, the lifeboats readied, watertight bulkheads shored up and one of the starboard-wing compartments flooded to try and keep the ship upright, her condition worsened as the flooding progressed. Using the starboard engine, Dampier tried to make a dash to Lough Swilly, but eventually it proved hopeless – *Audacious* 'was steering badly' and her electric power failed.

Olympic arrived on the scene late that morning along with several naval vessels. After Dampier requested that ships send their lifeboats, a number of *Audacious*' crew were successfully evacuated, including many who boarded *Olympic*. In an attempt to save *Audacious*, at Dampier's request HMS *Fury* helped pass a tow line to *Olympic* around 2 p.m. Although there was 'a considerable sea running', Dampier thought that 'the way in which the *Olympic* was handled was, in my opinion, a most excellent piece of seamanship.' She managed to turn *Audacious* from a westerly heading to the south-south-east in the direction of Lough Swilly. Unfortunately, despite Captain Haddock's best efforts, the tow parted as *Audacious* was 'quite unmanageable'. Another

Above: Two *Olympic* passengers, sisters Edith and Mabel Smith from Derby, witnessed the rescue of the *Audacious* crew by the ship's lifeboats. They also took a number of photographs showing the stricken vessel. Their brother, Charles Sydney Smith, was a Sherwood Forester officer then in camp at Plymouth. He expressed some disappointment in a letter to his fiancée Beatrice Slater, because Mabel had shown the photos to more than one publication to see whether they would be interested:

...therefore the photos are worth nothing like what they would have been had they been the only ones. However I managed to get £50 for them from the *Illustrated News* [sic]. £25 to be paid at once and the remaining £25 on publication, this is better than nothing, but I do wish Mabel had not been such a fool as to send prints to those two fellows as if they publish them it might make things awkward for me as I have sold these people the sole copyright and I should not want to get drawn into a law suit...

(Nigel Aspdin collection)

Right: The *Ocean Times* advised passengers of the precautions to take during wartime, which were issued on 17 October 1914. These and other similar instructions would have been in force during *Olympic*'s early commercial wartime voyages. (Author's collection)

SHIP'S NEWS

IMPORTANT NOTICE.

Passengers must take particular notice of the undermentioned, to assist the officers in securing the safety of the Ship:

DONT strike matches, smoke, or use flash-lamps, on deck after dark;

DONT take photographs. The use of cameras is prohibited by the "Defence of the Realm Act.";

DONT open ports or windows at sea. Your steward will attend to these;

DONT switch on any lights in your cabin except those actually required, and switch them off again when you leave;

DONT carry any letters or packages to or from the United Kingdom or the United States of America, for posting or delivery.

In the DANGER ZONE, wear or carry your life-belt; be warmly clad; and be ready for any emergency

In case of accident, a general alarm will be given by **Five Blasts on both Fog Whistles,** when you must go to your boat station; keep calm, and do what you are told by the ship's officers.

Gun firing practice, when necessary, will take place fifteen minutes after the lunch bugle has been blown, and Passengers must remain below.

attempt at towing failed, when the line was taken to HMS *Liverpool* and was cut when it fouled one of the ship's propellers. If Dampier had hoped that it was to be third time lucky, he was to be disappointed when a final attempt to tow using the collier *Thornhill* also ended in failure. By 5 p.m., the skies were darkening and *Audacious'* quarterdeck was awash. Dampier was the last to leave his ship and he boarded *Liverpool* so that he could remain close to his sinking ship until it was light.

Several hours later 'a terrific explosion occurred.' *Audacious*, increasingly unstable, turned bottom up and then sank stern first. The authorities had dispatched a telegram late that afternoon: 'Submit every endeavour should be made to keep *Audacious* incident from being published.' Meanwhile, a message from *Olympic* had also been intercepted, informing the White Star Line that she was standing by to assist *Audacious*; it was stopped and the authorities notified them confidentially instead. The failure to save the ship made it even more imperative. Instructions to the press were issued the same day, but while the government could censor the British media it could do little abroad.

Olympic had left once it was clear that there was no hope left for the stricken battleship. She proceeded to anchor in the relative safety of Lough Swilly. It was rather trying for Chief Surgeon John Beaumont, who was taken off the next day so that he could travel to Liverpool and transfer to *Baltic*. On arrival in New York, he felt 'besieged' by reporters' enquiries: 'Having been ordered by no less a personage than Admiral Jellicoe himself on board the *Iron Duke* that I was not to divulge anything to any one – not even to my own company – I obeyed to the letter. When I informed the press of New York that if any one on board my ship had given out the news that he had seen the battleship go down he was not telling the truth, I simply stated the facts of the case, for the *Audacious* did not go down till some hours after we had left her…'

The authorities did not want any of the ship's passengers landed at Lough Swilly. Fortunately, *Olympic* anchored out of sight of the fleet, hiding naval installations from prying eyes, yet there were two German-American passengers on board who could hardly be relied upon to keep the news confidential. The White Star Line were still worried about the danger from mines and *Olympic* did not leave Lough Swilly until 3.28 p.m. on 2 November 1914, arriving at Belfast the following day to land her passengers and then be laid up.

Although the cover-up was futile, since rumours spread and the ship's loss was reported in the American press, there were further frustrations for the British government as it became increasingly clear that the war would drag on. *Olympic* remained laid up at Belfast and, as the summer wore on, the authorities' interest in her increased. She was requisitioned as a troop ship and travelled to Liverpool, where she would leave for her first trip to the Mediterranean in September 1915.

BRITANNIC APPOINTMENTS

CAPTAIN: Charles Alfred Bartlett (14 December 1915; 4 September 1916)

ASSISTANT COMMANDER: Harry William Dyke (20 December 1915; 4 September 1916)

CHIEF OFFICER: Robert Hume (20 December 1915; 4 September 1916)

FIRST OFFICER: James Henry Callow (20 December 1915)
Hugh John Hollingsworth (4 September 1916)*
George Ernest Kemp Oliver (22 September 1916)

SECOND OFFICER: Alfred Brocklebank (20 December 1915; 4 September 1916)**

THIRD OFFICER: J.H. Walker (December 1915)
George Newlove (May 1916)
Francis W. Laws (September 1916)***

FOURTH OFFICER: J. J. Harris (December 1915)
Duncan Campbell McTavish (September 1916)

FIFTH OFFICER: W. Walker (December 1915)
Gordon Bell Fielding (6 September 1916)

SIXTH OFFICER: Duncan Campbell McTavish (December 1915)
John Chapman (September 1916)
Herbert R. Welsh (10 November 1916)

* Hollingsworth's subsequent transfer may have saved him from being on board when *Britannic* sank, but he went on to join *Justicia*. He survived her sinking in July 1918.
** In December 1915, *Britannic*'s log records the second officer's name as 'A. Brockehurst'; from September 1916, it is 'A. Brocklebank'. It is a mistake that has led to some confusion: the erroneous belief that two men sharing identical initials and similar names served as second officer at different times. In fact, Alfred Brocklebank's own career papers confirm that he served as second officer all along, and he was recorded on a crew list in May 1916.
*** Francis William is sometimes identified incorrectly as David Laws.

HMHS *BRITANNIC*

By the start of October 1915, the increasing demand for hospital ships in the Mediterranean had reached crisis point. One dispatch to the Admiralty reported that 'all hospitals at Mudros, Malta, Alexandria are quite full and no ships [are] available for clearing.' Even though Cunard's *Aquitania* had begun service as a hospital ship at the start of September 1915, with *Mauretania* following the next month, *Britannic* was needed more than ever. In late November 1915, one memo noted the potential demand for sixty hospital ships in Mediterranean service. *Britannic's* capacity was similar to that of eight smaller hospital ships, so her contribution would be invaluable.

HMHS *BRITANNIC*: JOHN RIDDELL'S ALBUM

★

Private John H. Riddell of the Royal Army Medical Corps (RAMC) was serving on board the hospital ship *Panama* when he took the chance to shoot several photographs of *Britannic* at Naples. Although blemished, they have a wonderful authentic quality and are unique images.

After arriving at Naples on 25 January 1916 to take on coal and water, *Britannic* was going to proceed once again to Mudros, but the Principal Naval Transport Officer at Cairo ordered her to remain where she was. She embarked 2,237 patients over a number of days from the hospital ships *Grantully Castle*, *Formosa*, *Essequibo*, *Nevasa* and *Panama*. The British authorities also took the chance to invite officers from the American warship *Des Moines* to inspect the ship, not to mention the American Ambassador to Rome, Nelson Page, as well as his wife and daughter. They wanted to demonstrate to the neutral country that *Britannic*, serving as a hospital ship, had nothing to hide. *Panama* came alongside *Britannic* on the morning of 4 February 1916 in order to transfer her 319 wounded for conveyance to Southampton. By 11.45 a.m., the process was completed and that afternoon *Britannic* was ready to sail. She left Naples at 3.15 p.m.

Riddell survived the war and his National Registration Identity Card confirms that he was still living at the end of May 1943.

Top left: John Riddell enjoys a cigarette. **Top right:** As *Britannic* gets ready to leave, her upper decks are crowded (one of the ship's motor launches can be seen aft on the boat deck). **Bottom left:** *Britannic's* starboard propeller begins to revolve (the mortuary can be seen above the ship's name and port of registry). **Centre right:** *Britannic* moves off. **Bottom right:** Vesuvius dwarfs the ship as it looms ahead of her. (Mark Chirnside/Michail Michailakis collection)

Although her interiors were incomplete, in May 1915 Harland & Wolff had advised Harold Sanderson that *Britannic's* engines had already undergone mooring trials. She could be made 'seaworthy in all respects' with accommodation fitted 'for officers, engineers and crew' in ten or twelve weeks. If the government assigned her priority, it would take four weeks. The shipyard got to work after it was confirmed that she would be required on 13 November 1915; she completed her sea trials on 8 December 1915 and left for Liverpool under Captain Joseph Ranson's command on the evening of 11 December 1915. The cost of her completion as a hospital ship was put at £90,000.

At Liverpool, additional work was needed to make her ready. (The contractors Messrs F.R. Butt & Co. had been told that *Britannic's* X-ray rooms would be ready by the end of November. They reported on 14 December 1915 that their representatives had found the 'X-ray rooms, wiring, etc. were not quite ready for the erection of the apparatus.') Meanwhile, a crew was assembled and preparations made for the maiden voyage. John Beaumont, appointed *Britannic's* chief surgeon, described her as:

> A fine vessel – the very latest word in everything new and the triumph of all that the science and art of modern shipbuilding could accomplish. The two large operating rooms, each with anaesthetic and instrument room attached; the X-ray rooms, dental cambers, dispensaries, research laboratories, lecture rooms, lofty and spacious wards to accommodate 4,000 [sic] sick and wounded; quarters for sixty doctors and 300 nurses, besides 800 of a ship's crew, galleys, staterooms, etc. all combined to make her a wonderful institution unsurpassed by any even on shore.

Her capacity was listed as 3,310 patients. She slipped out of Liverpool at 12.20 a.m. on 23 December 1915, bound for Mudros on the Greek island of Lemnos. It was a far cry from her sisters' maiden voyage departures.

Britannic took on 2,500 tons of coal and 1,500 tons of fresh water at Naples, arriving at Mudros on 31 December 1915, where she would see in the New Year. Beaumont was not a fan of the place: 'The island and mainland were bleak and forbidding, masses of barren rock, sand and mud on every side, no vegetation, lizards creeping around everywhere, few houses, but miles of tends and hospitals full of every fever…' Private Robert Edward Atkinson, among many wounded soldiers waiting to be taken home, remembered *Britannic's* arrival that afternoon. When the hospital ship *Egypt* came alongside to transfer him and others, she looked 'the size of a trawler' next to *Britannic*, 'although she has two funnels and is 12,000 tons.' On New Year's Day, around 10 a.m., he came aboard and found the largest British ship afloat (and the largest ship in service) an impressive sight:

> …from [fore] well deck into almost the bottom of this boat explore round and get lost. Five lots of stairs before reaching boat deck. Look down on [the hospital ship] *Dunluce* [*Castle*] appearing no bigger than trawler, other side SS *Egypt* looking just as small. Look up at the great height from engine room, electricians shop bells, detonators, telephones, lifts, swimming baths, just like a town, holding 6,000 patients [sic]… Top deck under cover like Crystal Palace the enormous width making a great hall… Stewards looking just as white and sickly as on other boats…

The next day, *Britannic* was still being loaded with potatoes and other goods. 'This monster still wants more to feed her,' Atkinson remarked. That evening, he attended church service, using the White Star Line's own gilt-edged prayer book. He was far from impressed with the meagre food rations. By 3 January 1916, still more wounded were coming aboard and Ward H was full. Atkinson searched for the library 'on aft staircase by lift and barber's shop. Chaplain as librarian.'

Finally, they left Mudros at 3.35 p.m. The first day's steaming encountered strong winds with 'waves washing up to our portholes'. *Britannic* passed through the Strait of Messina on 5 January 1916, logging 497 miles. Thirty-six boiler furnaces were unlit, with no more than twenty-one of

An excellent image of *Britannic*. It was taken later in her hospital ship career by Nurse H.K. Moore. (Imperial War Museum, HU 090768)

A rare view of *Britannic*, taking on wounded and medical supplies. The smaller hospital ship on the port side is hard to identify, but she may be one of the Union Castle ships. It is known that *Grantully Castle* and *Glenart Castle* came alongside during her fifth voyage, as well as a number of other vessels. (Digital restoration © Eric Keith Longo, 2011/Author's collection)

Eleven days later, she made a second round voyage, stopping only at Naples before she returned to Southampton. She was idle for weeks until a third round voyage, leaving Southampton on 20 March 1916, took her back to Naples and then Augusta in Sicily. Following her return to Southampton on 4 April 1916, she was moved to an anchorage off Cowes, but her future was less clear. As early as 16 January 1916, the War Office had requested that the three large hospital ships *Aquitania*, *Britannic* and *Mauretania* be discharged from service. By month's end, they had agreed to discharge a number of smaller vessels instead, as they would be useful on other services, but by 10 April 1916 both *Aquitania* and *Mauretania* had been discharged completely. The evacuation of the Dardanelles reduced the need for hospital ships.

Britannic's fittings remained intact, in case she was needed again, and the White Star Line were soon being paid the half-hire rate. After debate inside the government, she was discharged several days after she had returned to Belfast, on 21 May 1916. She was out of harm's way, but it was not to last. In July 1916, *Aquitania* was requisitioned; *Britannic*'s services were required as well. Harland & Wolff began reconverting her to a hospital ship on 24 July 1916. They engaged 'fitters and plumbers at the weekends' to try to

the ship's twenty-nine boilers in operation, and another run of 497 miles followed the next day. That evening, she passed Gibraltar at 9 p.m. Her best day's run increased to 512 miles as she passed Spain's Cape Finisterre. *Britannic* was quite capable of a steady twenty or 21 knots, while conserving fuel. On 8 January 1916 Atkinson got his khaki clothes ready and the ship came up the Solent the next day, Sunday.

Britannic docked at Southampton in the afternoon: 'See *Aquitania* funnels rising above the Church steeples of the town, six tugs: three in front pushing, three behind turning us, to get in dock. 3 p.m. start disembarking. 4,200 patients, each train holds 100 cases, we get on at 7 p.m. Waterloo 11 p.m. Hundreds of motors of gentlemen waiting for us, get in fine motor and off through the old familiar way, to Dulwich, Camberwell Infirmary under [the] name of Southwark Military Hospital.' Unlike her doomed sister, *Britannic* had safely completed her maiden voyage.

Another unusual view of *Britannic* 'shortly before [her] loss'. The smaller hospital ship bears a resemblance to the Union Castle's *Glenart Castle*. If that was the case, then it is known she came alongside *Britannic* on her fifth round voyage, the last time she was at Mudros. (Author's collection)

have her ready in time. Frank Tilbury, a Canadian soldier on board *Olympic*, wrote that *Britannic* was sighted at 6 a.m. on 29 August 1916. *Olympic* was off the southern Irish coast en route to Liverpool; *Britannic* was returning to Southampton to take on crew and supplies. On 9 September 1916 she was moved to an anchorage as she readied for her fourth voyage.

On 24 September 1916, Nurse Miss E. Barber described boarding a tender for *Britannic*'s fourth round trip to the Mediterranean:

> After a great deal of delay we finally left the docks and steamed down Southampton water to the *Britannic* which was lying at Bramble Buoy, off Cowes. We arrived onboard about 3.45 p.m. but all had to wait in the mess room on D-deck to sign our names in a book. We then were taken to our berths. Elliot, Sackville, Jones and I have four bunks together in the officers' ward on A deck. The curtains round our bunks can be pinned together and make a little room. The beds are of iron and riveted to the floor and they can be made to swing. We are very lucky in having big windows next to us and also plenty of bathrooms. I am almost blown out of bed in my bunk.

They had a cup of tea and biscuits and the stewards took their luggage up to their berths before dinner at 6 p.m. *Britannic* left Cowes twenty minutes beforehand and 'after dinner we went on deck and stayed there until we passed the Needles. We then went to bed about 8.30 p.m. (really 9.30 p.m. as the clock has been put back one hour).' Breakfast was served at 8 a.m. the following morning and she did not 'think we shall be left in peace for long as we have to go to a lifeboat drill at 11'. Nevertheless, she was impressed with the ship:

> There is the boat deck on top, where there is a gymnasium. We are not allowed there as it is reserved for the staff, which consists of a matron, Miss Dowse, who is an army sister, fairly old, a number of sisters and VADs [Voluntary Aid Detachment] and RAMC [Royal Army Medical Corps] officers and a chaplain.
>
> The deck we sit on is A deck. There are large officers' wards here, where we sleep, also a lounge & writing room. The theatres (2) are also on this deck. On B deck, the staff of the boat sleeps, in lovely cabins and there are wards for tommies. The dining saloon and nurses' sitting room is on this deck. Below C and D and E decks are all wards. There is an enormous room on D deck for convalescent patients to feed. From E deck you go down the gangway on to the launch or the tender. In F there is a swimming pool, which looks very jolly but we never eventually managed to bathe there. At night the Red Crosses on the sides of the ship are brightly lit up and all round there is a line of green light so that the hospital ships look lovely in the dark. There are always two meals. We

have ours first, and then the staff. The lifeboat practice was rather feeble we just put on lifebelts and strolled up to the boat deck. Today we have discovered that there is [sic] two sisters in charge of us. The head one is going to be somewhat severe and has already lectured us on manners!

Britannic reached the Bay of Biscay around 1 p.m. She felt 'the boat began to roll a bit, more so than usual, I should think, because it was so empty'. After sitting on deck all afternoon, she did not go down to dinner, but 'felt quite alright in the evening – I really felt rather pleased with myself as Jones and Rodwell and Elliot all succumbed'. By Tuesday, it was much calmer 'but still rolling a little. We sailed down the coast of Portugal fairly far out and could only see land at intervals. About 8 o'clock we passed quite close to Cape St. Vincent which rises sheer out of the sea. There was the most glorious sunset. In the evening the orderlies sang past songs very well on the lower deck.'

They reached Gibraltar very early the next morning but Captain Bartlett 'waited until it was light to be piloted through the minefield on the straights'. Her friend woke her up at 4.30 a.m. and a group of them went on deck. 'When it began to be light we moved round very slowly, right round the rock. The sun began to rise and the sea was perfectly smooth. A school of porpoises followed the boat for some time leaping in and out of the water in circles.'

Britannic arrived at Naples on Friday morning in heavy rain and mist, where the ship would take on coal and provisions. She had to pack up all her possessions as it had been expected that passengers on the way to Malta would be transhipped at Naples, but the plan changed and they would remain on board until Mudros. When she went ashore to do some sightseeing, 'we wanted to go to Pompeii but it was out of bounds for British troops and that apparently applied to us too'. (Perhaps they were unlucky on that particular day, since others saw Pompeii on the next voyage.) As the sun was setting, *Britannic* left Naples at 5.40 p.m. on Sunday: 'It was rather a stormy evening and the sunset on the clouds was lovely.' On Tuesday morning, the stewardess woke her earlier than usual as she wanted the nurses to get up so that their berths 'could be made up for patients'. The islands off Greece were in sight and by the afternoon *Britannic* was coming into Mudros:

> There were nine or ten hospital ships and a great many destroyers and cruisers. The *Britannic* stopped just outside a fine group and a little launch puffed up to us in the most funny way and signalled frantically, then darted away. After a little time it came back and evidently told us to proceed as we moved on right into the middle of the harbour. Before long, two hospital ships were towed up to us, one on each side. One was the *Warilda* which began to disembark wounded

from Salonika almost at once. The other, the *Galeka*, had brought wounded from Malta and we had orders to embark on it early the next morning. However whilst we were having dinner we received fresh orders to embark at once at 8 o'clock. We are only to be on it for two days and it is of course far smaller than the *Britannic*. We sleep in huge wards, about 45 beds in the one that I am in and there are two washbasins and no screens of any kind…

Meanwhile, after an efficient turnaround, at 9.51 a.m. on Thursday 5 October 1916 *Britannic* left for Southampton, where she arrived six days later. *Britannic* was already needed back at Mudros 'as soon as possible'. When she left Southampton on the afternoon of 20 October 1916, she carried 115 officers and 386 other ranks of the RAMC, as well as 161 nurses and 311 tons of

medical stores at the War Office's request. They would disembark at Mudros, en route to Egypt, Malta, Salonika, India and Mesopotamia. Although some questions had been raised about conveying medical personnel as passengers in hospital ships, the authorities decided to treat *Britannic* 'as a special case'. One official suggested that in future women might only be allowed: 'It would add to the safety of the women nurses and no question is likely to arise about the legality of conveying them.'

The round trip was successful and she was back at Southampton early in November 1916. This time, the turnaround took only six days rather than the previous trip's nine and she left Southampton shortly after noon on 12 November 1916. Once again, she was bound for Mudros via Naples, where she arrived five days later to take on coal and water.

BRITANNIC'S VOYAGES

DEPARTURE DATE		ARRIVAL DATE		DEPARTURE DATE		ARRIVAL DATE	
VOYAGE 1				7.30 p.m. 15 May 1916	Off Cowes	17 May 1916	Belfast
12.20 a.m. 23 December 1915	Liverpool	28 December 1915	Naples		Belfast		Southampton
3.5[1] p.m. 29 December 1915	Naples	31 December 1915	Mudros	9 September 1916	Southampton	9 September 1916	Off Cowes
3.35 p.m. 3 January 1916	Mudros	9 January 1916	Southampton				
				VOYAGE 4			
VOYAGE 2				5.40 p.m. 24 September 1916	Off Cowes	29 September 1916	Naples
11.51 a.m. 20 January 1916	Southampton	25 January 1916	Naples	5.40 p.m. 1 October 1916	Naples	3 October 1916	Mudros
3.15 p.m. 4 February 1916	Naples	9 February 1916	Southampton	9.51 a.m. 5 October 1916	Mudros	11 October 1916	Southampton
VOYAGE 3				**VOYAGE 5**			
4.26 p.m. 20 March 1916	Southampton	25 March 1916	Southampton	4.30 p.m. 20 October 1916	Southampton	25 October 1916	Naples
4 p.m. 27 March 1916	Naples	28 March 1916	Port Augusta	4.42 p.m. 26 October 1916	Naples	28 October 1916	Mudros
3 p.m. 30 March 1916	Port Augusta	4 April 1916	Southampton	12.05 p.m. 30 October 1916	Mudros	6 November 1916	Southampton
11 April 1916	Southampton	11 April 1916	Off Cowes	**VOYAGE 6**			
9 May 1916	Off Cowes	9 May 1916	Southampton	12.23 p.m. 12 November 1916	Southampton	17 November 1916	Naples
15 May 1916	Southampton	15 May 1916	Off Cowes	4.37 p.m. 19 November 1916	Naples	21 November 1916	'Ship sunk by enemy'

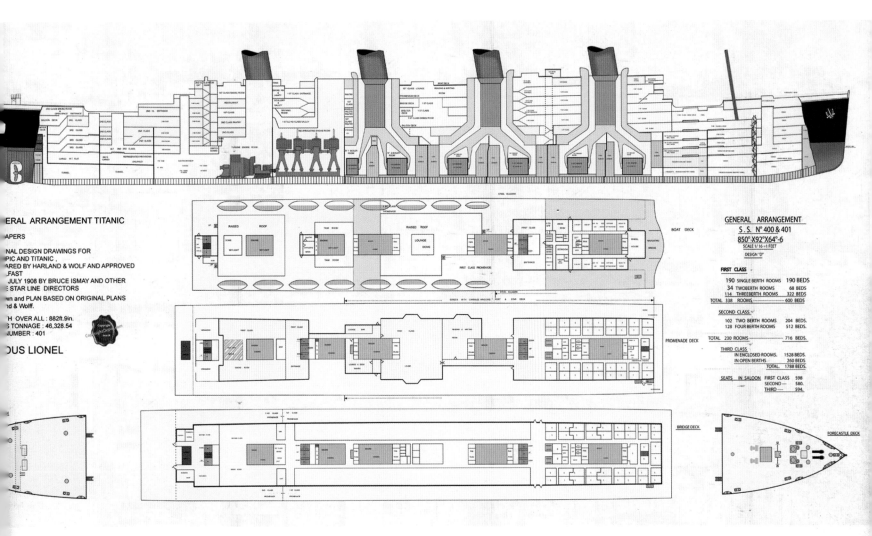

ERAL ARRANGEMENT TITANIC

APERS

NAL DESIGN DRAWINGS FOR
PIC AND TITANIC,
ARED BY HARLAND & WOLF AND APPROVED
FAST
JULY 1908 BY BRUCE ISMAY AND OTHER
E STAR LINE DIRECTORS

wn and PLAN BASED ON ORIGINAL PLANS
nd & Wolff.

H OVER ALL : 882ft.9in.
S TONNAGE : 46,328.54
NUMBER : 401

OUS LIONEL

GENERAL ARRANGEMENT
S. S. Nº 400 & 401
850' X92'X64'-6
SCALE 1/16 =1 FEET
DESIGN "D"

FIRST CLASS

190 SINGLE BERTH ROOMS   190 BEDS
34 TWO BERTH ROOMS   68 BEDS
114 THREE BERTH ROOMS   322 BEDS
TOTAL 338 ROOMS ————— 600 BEDS

SECOND CLASS

102 TWO BERTH ROOMS   204 BEDS.
128 FOUR BERTH ROOMS   512 BEDS.

TOTAL 230 ROOMS ————— 716 BEDS.

THIRD CLASS
IN ENCLOSED ROOMS.   1528 BEDS.
IN OPEN BERTHS   260 BEDS
TOTAL. 1788 BEDS.

SEATS IN SALOON   FIRST CLASS   598
SECOND ——   580.
THIRD   594.

By July 1908, Harland & Wolff had prepared a number of concepts including 'Design "D"' for *Olympic* and *Titanic*. It was approved in principle by the White Star Line. The builder's concept survives today at the Ulster Folk & Transport Museum and can be imagined using this plan drawn by the talented Lionel Codus. (Plan © Lionel Codus, 2011)

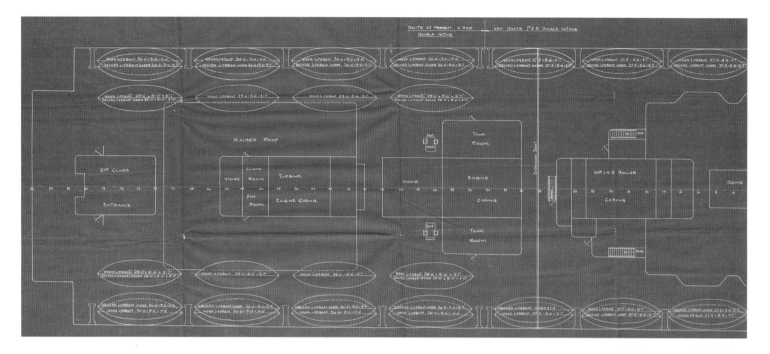

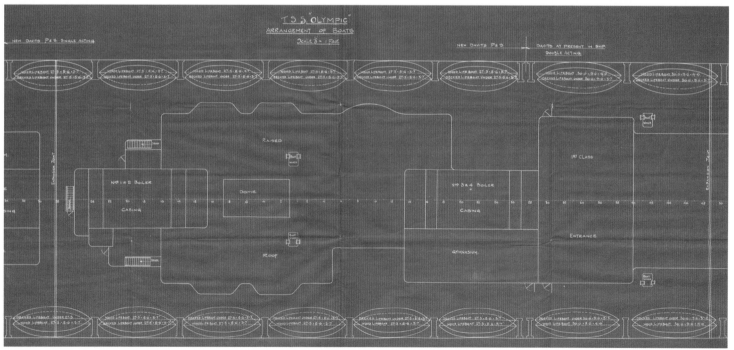

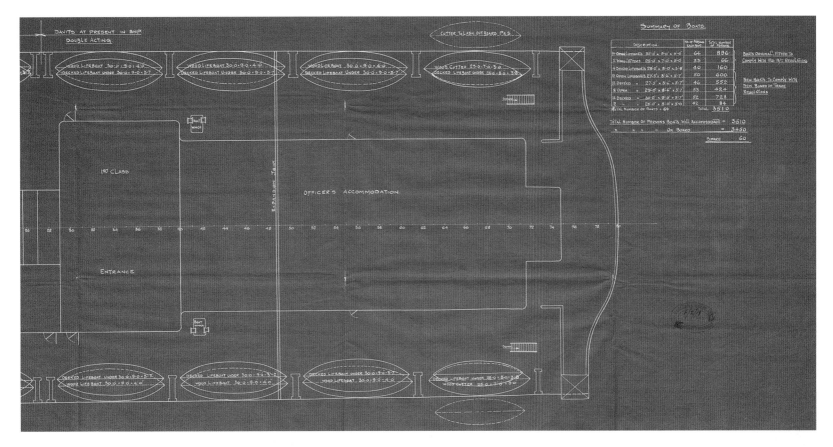

Opposite and above: The planned arrangement of *Olympic*'s sixty-eight lifeboats was shown in a plan by Harland & Wolff, stamped 6 February 1913. It is reproduced in three overlapping sections: the aft end of the boat deck (opposite top); the midship section (opposite bottom); and the fore boat deck and bridge (enlarged, above).

Contrary to popular belief, *Titanic*'s lifeboats were not reused on *Olympic*. They remained in New York until after *Olympic* returned to Belfast for her 1912–13 overhaul. It is also clear from the specifications that the 'new boats to comply with new Board of Trade regulations' were different in size to *Titanic*'s. However, due to supply problems the required boats were not all ready in time. On 11 March 1913 Harland & Wolff informed the Board of Trade that they would retain ten Berthon and six Henderson collapsibles on board as a temporary solution, while 'doing all possible to expedite the delivery of the remaining sixteen decked lifeboats' that would be 'placed onboard at the earliest possible opportunity'. (National Archives, United Kingdom)

70536 S. S. OLYMPIC ENTERING NEW YORK HARBOR ON FIRST TRIP.

Right: A pre-war postcard depicts *Olympic*'s maiden voyage arrival. (Author's collection)

WHITE STAR LINE R.M.S "OLYMPIC"
COMPARED WITH VARIOUS FAMOUS BUILDINGS.

Above: A popular method of showing off a vessel's great size was to compare her length to the height of well-known buildings. This card only shows *Olympic*, rather than *Olympic* and *Titanic*, which indicates it was post-1912. On the left-hand reverse side for correspondence was printed Warwick Arms Hotel, Warwick; about as far inland as one could get. (Author's collection)

Above: The twenty-three-year-old *Majestic* looked much smaller than her newer running mate *Olympic*, which was four and a half times her size measured by gross tonnage. (Author's collection)

Right: *Olympic*'s forward grand staircase: 'In the middle of the hall rises a gracefully curving staircase, its balustrade supported by light scroll work of iron with occasional touches of bronze, in the form of flowers and foliage. Above all a great dome of iron and glass throws a flood of light down the stairway, and on the landing beneath it a great carved panel gives its note of richness to the otherwise plain and massive construction of the wall. The panel contains a clock, on either side of which is a female figure, the whole symbolizing Honour and Glory crowning Time.' (Günter Bäbler collection)

The first-class reading and writing room as it appeared on board *Olympic* in 1911–12 and *Titanic* in 1912: 'The pure white walls and the light and elegant furniture show us that this is essentially a ladies' room… An atmosphere of refined retirement pervades the apartment; a homely fire burns in the cheerful grate; our feet move noiselessly over the thick, velvety carpet, and an arched opening leads to an inner recess – a sanctuary so very peaceful that here it would seem as if any conversation above a whisper would be sacrilege.' An independent observer's assessment was 'that the plan of this room and the windows and lighting, were considered excellent – particularly the lights above the boat deck.' (Author's collection)

Olympic's port side veranda café, which was a mirror image of the one on the starboard side. Passing through the revolving doors from the first-class smoke room, passengers emerged to see a 'verandah, over whose green trellis grow climbing plants, which foster the illusion that we are still on the fair, firm earth; but one glance through the windows, with their beautifully-chased bronze framing, adds to the charm, and we realise that we are still surrounded by the restless sea… Set in this flowery arbour are numerous inviting little tables, at which we can take our coffee or absinthe in the open air, much as we do in our own summery gardens on land…' (Author's collection)

"OLYMPIC" RESTAURANT.

Olympic's *á la carte* restaurant 'is of the Louis XVI period in design, and is panelled from floor to ceiling in beautifully marked French walnut of a delicate light fawn brown colour, the mouldings and ornaments being richly carved and gilded.' The 'floor is covered with a rich pile carpet of Axminster make, and a non-obtrusive design of the period in a delicate vieux rose, which forms an admirable background, and completed the harmonious ensemble. Comfort has been well considered in the arrangement of the room. It is furnished with small tables, to accommodate from two to eight persons, with crystal standard lamps and rose coloured shades to illuminate each table.' A report for Cunard in June 1911 noted 'that the general scheme upon this room was considered the best upon the vessel; that Mr Davis [of architects Messrs Mewes & Davis] thought the window treatment and the treatment of the transverse bulkheads well worth consideration for the public rooms of the *Aquitania*...' (Author's collection)

'Dignity and simplicity are the characteristics of the reception room,' advised the White Star Line. '... It is here that the saloon passengers will foregather for that important moment upon an oceangoing ship – *l'heure ou l'on dine* – to regale each other with their day's experiences in the racquet court, the gymnasium, the card room or the Turkish bath... Some of the passengers will stand to gaze at the magnificent tapestry directly facing the staircase, specially woven on the looms at Aubusson, or will await their friends seated upon the capacious Chesterfields or grandfather chairs upholstered in a floral pattern of wool damask, or the comfortable cane furniture distributed at intervals.' The room proved so popular that some passengers on *Olympic* even sat on the staircase while the orchestra was playing, as there were no more seats left. *Titanic*'s reception room was expanded by reducing the first-class entrance halls either side of the grand staircase and moving the foremost bulkhead. (J. Kent Layton collection)

Olympic's swimming pool was utilitarian in appearance and the White Star Line were unable to describe the magnificence of its décor. It was available for ladies and gentlemen at certain hours free of charge, and open at other times for a charge of 1s to passengers not booked for the Turkish baths. The pool was 33ft by 14ft, ranging from 4ft 5½in at the shallow end to 5ft 1½in at the deep end. The pool proved more popular with men than women during her first months in service. For Olympic's first three voyages, spring boards for diving were fitted, but experience showed it was dangerous because the water in the pool moved considerably even when the ship's motion was not that great. The marble steps proved too slippery and were eventually replaced with teak. (J. Kent Layton collection)

The cooling room of Olympic's Turkish bath establishment, 'one of the most interesting and striking rooms on the ship. The portholes are concealed by an elaborately carved Cairo curtain, through which the light fitfully reveals "something of the grandeur of the mysterious east".' It contained 'a handsome marble drinking fountain set in a frame of tiles'. (Daniel Klistorner collection)

Olympic's Adam-style sitting room, B39, could be found in the starboard side 'Parlour suite' on B-deck. Its counterpart on board *Titanic* was laid out slightly differently (see p.38). (J. Kent Layton collection)

One of the Harland & Wolff 'Bedroom B' staterooms, outfitted with oak dado and white panelling and equipped with a brass bed. A number of similar rooms were found amidships on B and C-deck. (J. Kent Layton collection)

The third-class general room was 'panelled and framed in pine and finished enamel white, with furniture of teak. This, as its name implies, will be the general rendezvous of the third-class passengers – men, women and children – and will doubtless prove one of the liveliest rooms in the ship... The new field of endeavour is looked forward to with hope and confidence, and in these vessels the interval between the old life and the new is spent under the happiest possible conditions...' (Günter Bäbler collection)

Leonard Peskett was keen to note a number of Olympic's interior features and submitted drawings of windows in the first-class veranda café, dining saloon, second-class smoke room and library. This particular first-class dining saloon arrangement (with a wall immediately beside the window) could not have been found on board the real ship. In fact, it was based upon a mock-up on shore, before the saloon was outfitted. (University of Liverpool Library, Cunard Archives)

GIGANTIC

'Some of the men on the White Star liner *Baltic* which arrived yesterday brought in a rumour that the line contemplates building another gigantic steamship of the same type and size as the *Titanic* and *Olympic*. The vessel will be built in the yards of Harland & Wolff, Belfast, and the rumour had it that the new vessel will be launched in 1913. She will be called the *Gigantic*,' the *New York Times* reported late in July 1911. Numerous reports appeared over the following months, giving the name of the new ship as *Gigantic*. The White Star Line do not appear to have made any public comment on the name, although it is known that J. Bruce Ismay had seen press reports and remarked that the ship's dimensions were not accurate. Following the *Titanic* disaster, in May 1912 the *Southampton Times* reported that Ismay had denied that the company or its management had ever intended to call the new ship *Gigantic*; and at the end of the month the name *Britannic* was reserved. Meanwhile, the *New York Times* reported that the name had been selected. The application was renewed on 1 June 1913 and confirmed when she was launched the following year.

Did the White Star Line ever intend to use the name *Gigantic*? There are plenty of reasons to suspect it. Cuthbert C. Pounder, a former director and chief technical engineer at Harland & Wolff, recalled in the late 1950s and early 1960s:

The original conception was three mammoth ships, bearing the names suitable for such vessels, namely: *Olympic*, *Titanic* and *Gigantic*. After the catastrophe which overtook *Titanic* on her maiden voyage in April 1912, it was decided to drop the name of the third vessel as it was felt that the public might be alarmed at the thought of travelling in a vessel the name of which was *Gigantic*, considering what had overtaken a vessel so large as to be called *Titanic*. The more conventional name *Britannic* was then substituted.

Pounder's statement is interesting, although he was speaking decades later and he was a young man in 1912. It is unlikely he knew first hand. Unlike her sister ships, *Britannic* was never the largest ship in the world. She could claim the honour of the largest British ship.

It kept cropping up over the years: it was reported that the company were going to build a new liner called *Gigantic*, in 1892; the advent of *Oceanic* prompted a report that 'the name *Gigantic* was considered, but it was finally determined to name her after their pioneer steam vessel, *Oceanic*,' in 1899; and *Olympic* might have been called 'the *Gigantic* were it not for the fact that the *Olympic*'s sister ship, also under construction, is to be named the *Titanic*. *Gigantic* and *Titanic* might sound just a trifle too boastful,' asserted one newspaper in October 1910. Nevertheless, the three names were very much in keeping, derived from Greek mythology.

Early in February 1912, *Engineering* reported that Harland & Wolff had placed an order with Messrs Andre Citroën and Co. for gearing equipment for the steering engines of a number of vessels, including *Gigantic*, as a result of 'the satisfactory working of the Citroën gears' on *Olympic*. Messrs Noah Hingley & Sons' chain and anchor order book contains reference to Yard Number 433, giving the name as *Gigantic* at 20 February 1912. Elsewhere, the company used the name as late as November 1913.

On the other hand, Edward Wilding stated that 'there is no name for twelve months', with a yard number being assigned to a ship before the name. This was not the case for *Olympic* and *Titanic*. Might it have been the case for their younger sister? Shortly after *Titanic* had left Southampton the *Shipbuilder* said the new ship had 'not been named.'

Tellingly, Harland & Wolff's order book shows only one name for the ship: that of *Britannic*.

Messrs Noah Hingley & Sons Ltd at Netherton, Dudley, recorded the order from Harland & Wolff for the anchor outfit for 'Yard Number 433' in their chain and anchor order book, which covered the period from August 1911 to June 1914. When the order was recorded in February 1912, the name *Gigantic* was given, but the company subsequently amended the name to *Britannic*. (Dudley Archives and Local History Service)

Harland & Wolff's own order book. The ship's breadth was originally intended to be the same as *Olympic* and *Titanic*'s but, by October 1911, it had been decided to increase it and this change was made in red ink. The increase in the length of the main boilers was noted and dated at 3 January 1912. The yard number, name *Britannic*, and original specifications were all included in the entry and there is no evidence that these details were written at different times. They were recorded before the ship's keel was laid and only include the name *Britannic*. (Public Records Office Northern Ireland/Harland & Wolff)

WHITE STAR LINE R.M.S. BRITANNIC 50000 TONS ON THE STOCKS

Above and opposite: Two colour postcards issued to celebrate *Britannic*'s launch
reflected similar photographs taken of the ship 'on the stocks' and 'leaving the ways'.
(Author's collection)

WHITE STAR LINE R.M.S. "BRITANNIC" – 50,000 TONS – LEAVING THE WAYS

(Digital restoration by James Samwell, © 2011/Author's collection)

A striking artist's impression on a postcard which depicted how the new ship would appear in service. (Author's collection)

R.M.S. Britannic
Length, 900 ft.
Breadth, 94 ft.
Tonnage, 50,000

Another similar view, on a postcard. There may be debate as to the precise colour of White Star 'buff' – below the black funnel tops – but the ship's funnels are quite distinctive. (Ioannis Georgiou collection)

The front cover of an authentic publication commemorating the launch of 'the new *Britannic*… both in design and construction, as perfect a specimen of man's creative power as it is possible to conceive.' (Digital restoration by James Samwell, © 2011/ Ioannis Georgiou collection)

It included a remarkable view of the new steamer at high speed, her powerful engines generating enough power to propel her through the water at about 27 land miles per hour. (Digital restoration by James Samwell, © 2011/ Ioannis Georgiou collection)

In a cropped extract from a larger, damaged illustration, *Britannic* appeared on the cover of a leaflet advertising the many services offered by IMM's constituent lines. Passengers can be seen on the forward end of A and B-deck. (Author's collection)

BRITANNIC'S ORGAN

Contrary to popular myth, *Titanic* did not have an organ installed. However, her younger sister's fittings were even grander and the White Star Line planned for one as a proud feature of her luxurious first-class accommodation. The original plan seems to have envisaged an organ from the Aeolian Company, however as the ship's outfit was finalised this changed.

Britannic's patriotic name and her status as the largest British ship did not deter the company from placing an order for the largest Philharmonie organ (or Philharmonic, meaning that it had a keyboard) that was available from the firm of Welte, at Freiburg in Germany. An organist could play it, or alternatively an automatic mechanism could be employed to play pre-recorded music using perforated paper music rolls. Welte's famous customers included Winston Churchill and, as David Rumsey writes, 'only individuals or corporations with superior wealth could ever hope to possess one' of the company's instruments. The model was not ready to be offered for sale until towards the end of 1912 and the indications are all in agreement that *Britannic*'s organ was ordered, planned and built at Freiburg the following year. It would be a remarkable and impressive feature of the new ship.

When she entered service, *Olympic*'s orchestra did not play at lunch or dinner, instead playing at set times in different locations:

10 a.m. to 11 a.m.	Second-class entrance
11 a.m. to 12 p.m.	First-class boat deck entrance
4 p.m. to 5 p.m.	First-class reception room
5 p.m. to 6 p.m.	Second-class entrance
8 p.m. to 9.15 p.m.	First-class reception room
9.15 p.m. to 10.15 p.m.	Second-class entrance

Perhaps *Britannic*'s organ, whose music would be heard throughout the landings of the grand staircase, would have been available to play as first-class passengers went down to dinner.

Was the organ ever installed? If it had not been delivered to Belfast already, the outbreak of war in August 1914 stopped any prospect of it being shipped from Germany. The ship had not been expected to enter passenger service until the spring of 1915, so her interiors were far from complete five months after launching. Nor does it seem likely that it would have been installed once she was being fitted out as a hospital ship or while she was out of service in the summer of 1916. After the ship's loss, a Steinway piano was mistakenly included in her total cost, which was the basis of compensation from the government. The White Star Line realised the mistake and offered to purchase it back for £45 unless the Admiralty had any use for it. However, there seems no documentation or trace of the grander organ being among the ship's remaining fittings which had been stored ashore and were auctioned off after the war. In all likelihood, it never left Germany.

The organ was installed in camera manufacturer August Nagel's Stuttgart home in 1920, before being returned to the Welte company and installed in the reception room of the Radium lighting company in 1937, where it was in use until the 1960s. Heinrich Weiss, who founded the Swiss Museum für Musikautomaten in Seewen, acquired it and moved it in 1969–70. It was fully restored at its new home at the Swiss National Museum, Seewen, in 2007. It is now used in the regular museum guided tours and is central to a nationally funded Swiss research project, *Wie von Geisterhand* ('as played by the hand of a ghost') into musical performance practises of the early twentieth century as revealed by player organ rolls.

Above: The intricate pipework inside the organ. (Museum für Musikautomaten, Seewen, Switzerland)

Above right: the organ's console and roll playing mechanism during restoration. (Museum für Musikautomaten, Seewen, Switzerland)

Right: A magnificent view of the completed organ in the museum's Klangkunstsaal in October 2007. (Museum für Musikautomaten, Seewen, Switzerland)

Far left: A period illustration from a Welte catalogue showing an organ installed on a large British liner leaves little doubt that the vessel was *Britannic.* (Günter Bäbler collection).

Left: A telltale marking incorrectly spells *Britannic*'s name, including substituting the German 'k' for 'c'. (Museum für Musikautomaten, Seewen, Switzerland)

H. M. S. "Hawke"

Left: Some 360ft long by 60ft in breadth, HMS *Hawke* had a total complement of 530. Famous for her collision with *Olympic* in 1911, she became one of the war's early casualties when she was torpedoed in the North Sea in the middle of October 1914. (Author's collection)

Below: This detailed side elevation and overhead view, by the talented artist Cyril Codus, depicts *Britannic* in her hospital ship configuration. (Plan © Cyril Codus, 2007–11)

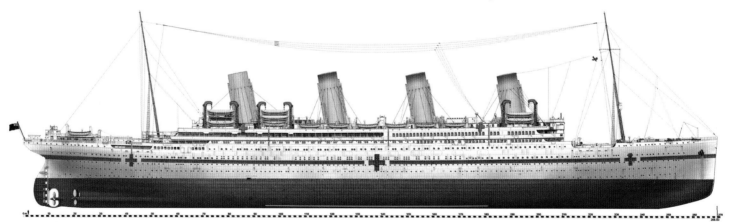

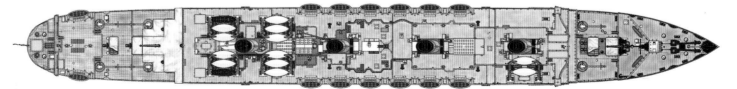

HMHS / BRITANNIC

PLAN ARTISTIQUE EN COULEUR DU HMHS/BRITANNIC
PLAN REALISE PAR : CYRIL CODUS
ECHELLE : 1/135
ANNEE : 2007   Copyright © France-

Right: An *Olympic* postcard, sent in October 1918, describing the ship on the reverse as 'a wonderful achievement of British shipbuilding'. (Author's collection)

R.M.S. "OLYMPIC. 46,359 TONS
(The largest British Steamer)
Viewed from a Seaplane whilst on War Service

Left: An aerial illustration of *Olympic* at sea, based upon a photograph now held at the Imperial War Museum, London. (Author's collection)

Below: Arthur Lismer's famous painting of *Olympic* at Halifax: *Olympic With Returned Soldiers*, completed in 1919. In contrast with the aerial illustration, Lismer's depiction accurately portrays the colours used: mixtures of grey, cream and blues, rather than the bright blues, reds and yellows. (Canadian War Museum, CWM19710261-0343)

A BODY BLOW

On the morning of Tuesday 21 November 1916, in fine weather and smooth seas, *Britannic* was maintaining a moderate 20 knots. At 7.52 a.m. her course was changed so that she was heading north-east through the Kea Channel on the way to Mudros. Chief Officer Robert Hume was on the bridge with Fourth Officer Duncan McTavish. Forty-three-year-old Hume had risen through the ranks, from serving as second officer on *Olympic*'s maiden voyage to becoming chief officer when *Britannic* sailed. No doubt twenty-six-year-old McTavish was still enjoying his promotion from *Britannic*'s sixth to fourth officer. Fifteen-year-old James Vickers, one of the scouts, heard Hume remark upon 'the large number of small Greek boats in the area. This had never been seen on previous voyages.'[1]

The tranquil scene was shattered at 8.12 a.m. There was a 'tremendous but muffled explosion... the ship trembling and vibrating most violently fore and aft, continuing for some time; the ship fell off about three points [an angle over 33 degrees] from her course.' The force was such that water was thrown as high as D-deck by the explosion 'and a cloud of black smoke was seen, the fumes for some time being suffocating'.

Bert Smith, in boiler room 6, had just come on watch. After hearing what seemed to be a loud bang followed by a massive explosion, he headed towards the entrance to the firemen's tunnel. He was met by a rush of water which pinned him against one of the boilers. He was knocked over, but made his way up to safety. Only the previous month, he had been on board the hospital ship *Galeka* when she struck a mine and his wartime adventures were not over yet. Private J.W. Cuthbertson was alone in the forward barrack room on G-deck. His escape sounded miraculous, since the staircase was blown away and the room flooded very quickly.

Captain Rentoul assembled the nurses amidships with lifejackets and blankets, ready for them to board lifeboats; Lieutenant Shekleton had charge of the only patients on board (a number of men from the

Below: *Britannic*'s bow: the forepeak, hold 1, hold 2, hold 3, boiler room 6 and boiler room 5. The explosion took place 'on the starboard side low down and in the vicinity of the bulkhead between 2 and 3 holds', which filled those two compartments; it is unclear if the bulkhead to number 1 hold was compromised, but that compartment flooded as well, perhaps through the flooding firemen's tunnel; the tunnel also allowed water into boiler room 6, through the open watertight door which failed to close. The door leading to boiler room 5 was only partially closed. The forepeak would have flooded as the bow settled lower in the water. Even in this condition, with six major compartments flooded and her bow submerged *Britannic* should have survived: the watertight door to boiler room 4 was closed and there is no evidence that water penetrated that far from low down in the ship. Unfortunately, another complication sealed the ship's fate.

About fifteen minutes after the explosion, the portholes on E-deck 'on a line between the first and second funnels were awash and water was coming along this deck from forward'. Fifth Officer Gordon Fielding described: 'Owing to the fact that the portholes... all along the sides of the ship were open to allow thorough ventilation for the wounded we were to take onboard the same night, it was impossible to stop the rush of the sea through these holes... the watertight bulkheads were now useless.' The open portholes allowed flooding aft of the critical watertight bulkhead which separated boiler rooms 5 and 4. (Digital amendment of the watertight bulkheads by Mark Chirnside, © 2011/J. Kent Layton collection)

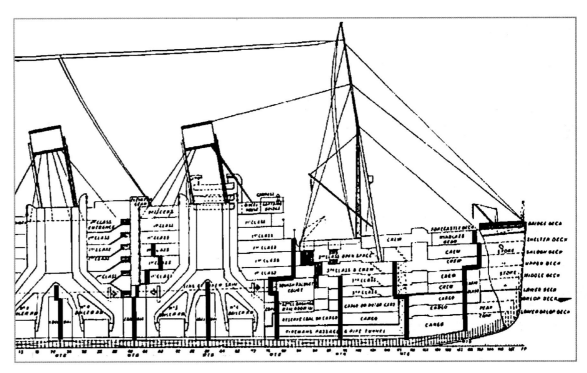

RAMC) and assembled them on the boat deck; Major Priestley saw his men paraded with their lifejackets aft on A-deck, before going below and searching the three after barrack rooms on F and G-deck. Scout Henry Pope reported to his station, assisting Purser Claude Lancaster. He remarked: 'It's been a big explosion, sir, but I don't think it's done us much harm.'

Nurse W. Greenwood recalled: 'Just as we sat down to breakfast, there was a terrific crash which shook the ship from end to end. Everybody stood up at once, but I heard no one speak, for some seconds, then an officer said: "Keep your seats, it's alright".' Some minutes later, they got their lifebelts and headed for the boat deck: 'The crew were working with frantic speed swinging out lifeboats…'

Captain Bartlett did not panic. His first impression was that his ship had struck a mine and would survive. He sounded the alarm, ordered the engines stopped, the watertight doors closed and the transmission of an SOS signal: 'I gave orders to clear away all boats and have all possible ready to be sent away.' The ship's master at arms, Mr B. Coe, arrived and reported that he thought 'that a torpedo had entered No.1 RAMC barrack room' and the first hold was flooding. Bartlett decided to try to manoeuvre so that she could be beached. Unfortunately, *Britannic* had begun to develop a list to starboard and the 'steering gear appeared to have failed': 'I turned [the] ship round to port to head for land by the engines, but the forward holds filled rapidly and water was reported in Nos 5 and 6 boiler rooms, so I stopped the engines and ordered all boats possible to be sent away, but to stand by near the ship.'

Britannic's fifth officer, Gordon Fielding, had been in his room shaving when 'the boat lifted twice, and everything seemed to dance'.[2] The twenty-four-year-old Yorkshireman with brown hair and blue eyes threw his uniform onto his 5ft 10in frame and rushed to his boat station at the after end of the boat deck on the port side. He immediately swung out two of the lifeboats 'which were promptly rushed by the stewards' and then a dozen seamen, who were needed to launch the lifeboats. It was a sudden panic and he persuaded the seamen to come back on board, taking the opportunity to get the stewards out of the way by lowering the boats to within 6ft of the water. He did not release them as the ship's engines were still being used, and the order from the bridge not to release any boats confirmed his wise precaution.

Two of the lifeboats under Third Officer Francis Laws' charge had been released without his knowledge and Fielding later estimated that they 'must have dropped some 6ft into the water, they must have been stove in…' Eyewitness accounts vary, but the consequences were certainly fatal: *Britannic*'s port propeller was rotating above the surface and two boats were promptly smashed. Some people managed to jump overboard and escape; others were killed by the powerful blades. By chance, as a third boat was pulled towards it the propeller came to a stop. A number of its occupants had already jumped out. Captain T. Fearnhead of the RAMC was one of three people left. They pushed against the blade of the propeller in order to move the boat away.

Fielding was all too aware of the increasing list *Britannic* was taking to starboard, as the bow sank lower. Bartlett had given the order to abandon ship and the ship's officers and crew worked tirelessly. He lowered his first two boats to the water, but the forward pair of giant 'girder' davits at his station were no longer in use; on the release of a third boat, he readied the motor boat. First Officer George Oliver approached and explained that he had been asked to take charge of it. The thirty-nine-year-old was experiencing his second shipwreck. He had been on board White Star's *Arabic* when she went down very quickly in August 1915.

Fielding lowered the port side motor launch around 8.45 a.m. Lieutenant Colonel H.S. Anderson, *Britannic*'s officer commanding troops, was also on board and helped rescue survivors from the wrecked lifeboats in the water. The starboard launch and other boats were close by, but the sinking ship's forward momentum had carried her some distance away. Bartlett 'passed word to stop lowering boats' and started the engines again in a final attempt to work *Britannic* towards the shore. She became increasingly unmanageable and the centre propeller was soon working above the surface.

Although one final boat was lowered from the port side, it 'very nearly capsized a few times'. Fielding, together with thirty men of the RAMC and about six seamen, threw collapsible rafts and deckchairs over the starboard side from the middle of the boat deck. Sixth Officer Herbert Welsh, who had

DEPARTURE OF N. HIGHLAND BRIGADE
S.S. OLYMPIC.

Left: By the autumn of 1915, Cunard's *Aquitania* was serving as a hospital ship and *Olympic* was in service as a troopship. They are seen here at Mudros. (Author's collection)

Above: *Olympic*'s paintwork shows signs of wear as she gets ready to depart Halifax. (From the collection of the Maritime Museum of the Atlantic)

joined the ship only eleven days earlier and overseen the launch of ten boats, was at a smaller boat with several seamen. Fielding and his men helped to lower it. When it was in the water, two seamen slithered down the falls and then Fielding followed. It appeared to him as though '*Britannic* was toppling over on top of us', but they got clear astern.

Major Priestley remained until the end, jettisoning rafts as well and making sure everyone had left. It was only when Purser Claude Lancaster called him to the last lifeboat at 9 a.m. that he left, and even then he made sure that the eight RAMC men with him boarded it first. James Vickers, who had watched

THE OCEAN TIMES
AND
THE ATLANTIC DAILY NEWS
News received daily by wireless telegraphy

Price: 10 Cents (5d.) Presented gratis by the White Star Line, the Holland-America Line, the Scandinavian American Line, the Compagnie Générale Transatlantique, the Royal Holland Lloyd, the Compagnie Belge, the Navigazione Generale Italiana, the Veloce and the Lloyd Italiano.

WHITE STAR LINE

ROYAL AND UNITED STATES MAIL SERVICE
SOUTHAMPTON —— CHERBOURG —— NEW YORK

(Calling at Plymouth, EASTBOUND)
WEDNESDAYS

(This Service is temporarily suspended owing to War Conditions.)

"OLYMPIC," 46,359 tons, IS THE LARGEST BRITISH STEAMER.

REGULAR PASSENGER AND FREIGHT SERVICES

—————— *from* LIVERPOOL *to* ——————

NEW YORK.   BOSTON.   QUEBEC.   MONTREAL.
HALIFAX (N.S.) PORTLAND. CAPE TOWN. AUSTRALIA.

LONDON TO CAPE TOWN AND NEW ZEALAND.
NEW YORK AND BOSTON TO MEDITERRANEAN.

THE SERVICES AND CONNECTIONS OF THE WHITE STAR LINE ENCIRCLE THE GLOBE.

WHITE STAR LINE | 30, JAMES STREET, LIVERPOOL.
1, COCKSPUR STREET, S.W., } LONDON.
38, LEADENHALL STREET, E.C., }
CANUTE ROAD, SOUTHAMPTON.
N. MARTIN AGENT, 9, RUE SCRIBE, PARIS.

Left: On 11 February 1918, the cover of *The Ocean Times* advised that the White Star Line's Southampton to New York express 'service is temporarily suspended owing to war conditions'. (Author's collection)

Right: Workmen apply 'dazzle' paint to *Olympic*'s side. The paint scheme was first applied to *Olympic* in the late summer of 1917. In Wilkinson's words, 'Dazzle painting is a method to produce an effect (by paint) in such a way that all accepted forms of a ship are broken up by masses of strongly contrasted colour, consequently making it a matter of difficulty for a submarine to decide on the exact course of the vessel to be attacked.' The purpose was not to make the ship invisible. (*Illustrated London News*, 1919/Author's collection)

with increasing concern as the bow settled deeper into the water, was firmly ordered 'off the bridge' by Captain Bartlett: 'I was able to get into the last lifeboat.'

Any lingering hopes that *Britannic* would be saved vanished. When he had restarted the engines, Bartlett noted that she had 'seemed to stop settling a little', but 'she again seemed to settle rapidly' and water was reported on D-deck. The ship's bow was now completely submerged. Bartlett gave the final order to abandon ship and blew the whistle for the last alarm. As he signalled 'finished with engines' on the engine room telegraphs, he was surprised to receive an acknowledgement from the engine room:

> The ship was sinking very quickly then, going by the head and listing to starboard and soon the water came to the bridge and Assistant Commander Dyke having reported to me that all had left, I told him to go and shortly after followed myself, walking into the water by the forward boat gantry on starboard side, the third funnel falling a few minutes later.

Chief Engineer Robert Fleming, Assistant Chief Engineer Joseph Wolfe and their colleagues remained at their posts until the end. Wolfe recalled his escape: 'When we reached the deck the foremost of the four funnels was touching the water, and the bows were completely

caused by the port propeller breaking the surface. He ordered both motor boats to proceed to Port St. Nikolo with the injured, passing word for the other boats to follow. As they made their way there, the naval vessels *Heroic* and *Scourge* could already be seen approaching. They and other vessels 'did splendid work in picking up the boats and then proceeded to Piraeus with the rescued'.

Following the rescue, other heroic tales emerged. Captain E.G. Fenton, who knew from a previous shipwreck that he would occupy the space of two people in a lifeboat, climbed over the ship's side and down one of the falls, even though he had little experience of climbing or swimming. *Britannic*'s scouts, employed as signallers, messengers and lift boys, all 'behaved splendidly throughout'. Scout J.H. Price accompanied Chief Officer Hume during the evacuation and communicated his orders by megaphone. Captain Bartlett recalled Edward Ireland:

submerged. We jumped eighty feet into the sea from the second-class quarters on C-deck and after swimming clear we watched the awesome sight of the mighty liner sinking.' Lieutenant Starkie had been below to fetch as much bread as possible. On his return, he found the bridge was submerged as water washed up the boat deck. He had only swum out 100 yards, using his best front crawl, when *Britannic* disappeared.

'She went down bows first until she reached the first deck,' Nurse Ada Garland remembered, 'when she keeled over on her starboard side and as each of her four funnels touched the water they smashed off like matchwood. It was as if she was a pitiful demure animal, tortured, her sirens blasting for help up to the last. In just 50 minutes [sic] she disappeared, nothing left but wreckage, boats battered and overturned told their own tale – there was nothing we could do but pray.' It was 9.07 a.m.

Bartlett watched his ship founder and was picked up by one of the motor launches. It was only then that he found out about the fatalities

He was attached to the bridge at the time of the explosion and he remained at his post until I sent him away finally with the quartermaster, although on several occasions I had told him to go to the boats. He was of great service in telephoning my orders, and I have great admiration for the pluck he showed in standing by with the prospect in front of him of eventually going down with the ship.

Bartlett hoped that the Boy Scouts Association would give Ireland a recognition to value 'forever'. He was awarded the Cornwell Decoration and subsequently joined the Royal Air Force. His short life ended when he was killed in an aeroplane accident on 31 July 1919.

MINE OR TORPEDO?

Rumours circulated as to whether *Britannic* had been struck by a mine or a torpedo. Perhaps it was the authorities who were most keen to establish what had happened, since a torpedo would have been a deliberate attack on a hospital ship by the enemy, whereas a mine did not distinguish what sort of vessel it wounded.

Captain Bartlett's first impression was that they had 'struck a mine'. There is no record of any of the lookouts, or officers on the bridge, sighting a torpedo track or the enormous column of water that would have been the inevitable consequence of a torpedo hit. However, as Bartlett mentioned in his report on the ship's loss, and as the commanding officers of HMS *Duncan* recorded, there were several witnesses who thought otherwise.

Thomas Walters, a deck steward, was standing on the starboard side of A-deck 'looking over the rail in a forward position when my eyes caught sight of a white stream coming at a great speed towards the ship's bow. The thought flashed to my brain that this was a torpedo on the instant I gripped the rail and leaned inboard to await the explosion which seemed to occur immediately I then looked down at the water but had to hold my nostrils on account of the fumes which were stifling. I could see what appeared to be a great disturbance of water aft.'

One of the ship's bakers, Henry Etches, complicated the situation. He was on the poop deck when the explosion occurred and rushed to the port side. He reported seeing a torpedo track: 'a long straight line following it reaching as far as my eye could follow…'

Twenty minutes after the explosion, Thomas Eckett was on the starboard side of the poop deck alongside lifeboat number 19. He saw what he thought was a submarine and commented to Fireman E. Biffen, who was standing next to him, that 'it looked as if the submarine had come up to shell us'. After two minutes, it was submerging: 'there was not the smallest of waves breaking, it was this smoothness of the sea that enabled me to note the wash and wake of the object so plainly, compelling me to conclude that it must be a submarine.'

Walters, who had served as an officer's steward in the navy and witnessed torpedo practice, could not be dismissed easily, but the sightings on each side of the ship indicated two torpedoes and it must have seemed highly unlikely that two submarines could have attacked the ship simultaneously. The tell-tale water column was missing. The report into the ship's sinking concluded: 'The effects of the explosion might have been due to either a mine or torpedo. The probability seems to be a mine.'

It is now known that Gustav Siess' *U73* had laid a number of mines in the Kea Channel on 28 October 1916. In fact, the last mine of a barrier of six mines was less than half a mile to the south east of where *Britannic* went down. When he learned of the ship's loss, Siess concluded she had struck one of his mines and claimed her in his count of tonnage sunk.

'OLD RELIABLE'

Since she was employed as a troopship rather than a hospital ship, in theory *Olympic* was in more danger than *Britannic* had been. Although she suffered many narrow escapes, her war service was a considerable success. Corporal Frank Leslie Stone remembered *Olympic*'s first trooping voyage. He thought it was rough going through the Bay of Biscay: 'Everybody was ill. The boat got in a terrible state, and the stench was awful… The food was very poor, and the drinking water always lukewarm.' By 27 September 1915, he was feeling a bit better, but in the evening he was designated in charge of one of the watertight doors. 'Mine was the best door, being close to the officers' quarters and away from the awful crowd and smell.' Stone remembered swimming in *Olympic*'s pool, as 'it was more than a treat!' On the morning of 1 October 1915 the French steamer *Provincia* had been sunk and Stone remembered two small boats were sighted with men aboard: 'We stopped and picked them up.' After parade that afternoon, 'we were startled by hearing two shots – soon after this, the alarm sounded and off we rushed to our alarm post – it appears a submarine came in view and was fired on, but not before it had fired a torpedo which missed us by about fifty yards – we were then dismissed.' Captain Hayes described the torpedo passing astern in his memoirs ten years later, as did other troops on board, yet *U33*'s log did not mention firing one and there were no other German submarines nearby. *Olympic*'s log only recorded sighting the submarine and taking evasive action: 'steered various courses until dusk…' The French authorities were glad to award a medal to Hayes, but although all had ended well the British authorities felt that 'although prompted no doubt by the highest motives [this rescue action] was dangerous, as the *Olympic* had 6,000 troops on board at the time'. Fortunately, *Olympic* arrived safely at Mudros. The bay 'was full of every kind of sea craft', Stone wrote. On another occasion, *Olympic*'s final voyage to Mudros was interrupted by a plane from Bulgaria which dropped several bombs, missing the ship as they splashed into the water around her.

On the morning of 23 February 1916, *Olympic* was well on her way to Mudros. Second Officer Alfred Herbert Fry was on the bridge. (He had been appointed to *Olympic* on 3 April 1912 and, after serving on board other liners, rejoined in September 1915. Surely, with the benefit of hindsight, he considered himself fortunate to have been transferred to *Olympic* in early April 1912, rather than her doomed sister.) Just as the ship's course had been altered, the quartermaster on the port wing of the bridge drew his attention to an object flashing in the sun. When Fry examined it with his binoculars, he realised it was a submarine's periscope. Ordering the helm hard a port, he directed the guns to open fire. Although several rounds were fired, they were unable to get a direct hit on the submarine: 'all the gunlayer could see to fire at was something shining in the sun and troubled water.' It was a lucky escape. The submarine turned out to be Lieutenant Commander Lothar

Olympic's longest serving commander, Captain Bertram Fox Hayes. As she returned from New York to Southampton early on the morning of 12 May 1918, a submarine was spotted; *Olympic*'s forward gun missed it. In Hayes' words: 'We put our helm hard a port again, and at 3.55 a.m. hit him a swinging blow with our stem which put an end to his career.' The impact 'jumped us off our feet on the bridge'. *U103* foundered, but four officers and twenty-seven men were picked up by the American *Davis*. (From the collection of the Maritime Museum of the Atlantic)

Left: On 3 August 1918, *Olympic* was photographed at New York looking heavily weathered. She is in the first version of her dazzle paint schemes (type 19, design A). It is interesting to note that the hull plating alongside the fore well deck has been cut away and replaced by open railings. Coaling vessels are alongside, while the fourteen lifeboats that have been swung out represented a mere fraction of the huge number required in trooping service. (United States National Archives and Records Administration)

Below left: Another view, taken the same day and showing the stern. The two small drums on the platform overhanging the stern are smoke floats, intended for use if the ship was being chased by an enemy. (United States National Archives and Records Administration)

von Arnauld de la Periere's *U35*, which had seen *Olympic* but was unable to mount an attack. Five days later, the Admiralty believed that the prolific German commander had attacked *Olympic*, but his log made no mention of seeing her. *Olympic*, on the other hand, logged the sighting of a 'submarine above water, near to 2 masted and 1 funnel steamer,' which was relayed to a naval vessel. Once again her luck held. She returned from her final voyage to the Mediterranean unscathed.

Olympic left Liverpool for her first trooping run to Halifax, arriving in the Canadian port on 28 March 1916. In Captain Hayes' words, 'Halifax would become a "home from home" to ship's company... I shall never forget the kindness and hospitality that I received... and I don't think that any member of the crew will either; we were received with open arms...'[3] It was the first of ten round trips she would make to Halifax in 1916 alone. The routine on board is described in a few extracts from Lieutenant Colonel W.J. Green's report, 'War Diary of O.C. [Officer Commanding] Troops, HMT 2810,' in the summer of 1916:

WEDNESDAY, 28 June 1916

Troops began embarking early this morning…

Officers commanding units and drafts were assembled at 8 p.m. of this date to receive Standing Orders…

THURSDAY 29 June 1916

The officer commanding troops made a complete inspection of the ship and found that the routine of messing and fatigues, although not working perfectly, was well in hand. Unfamiliarity with their surroundings by the troops was in a large measure responsible for the lack of order and cleanliness.

Routine orders for the day were issued by the officer commanding troops in which his staff was properly appointed.

Life belts were drawn and all men properly instructed as to the wearing of the same before 7 p.m.

A lecture was delivered by the ship's sergeant major to the senior sergeants of the units onboard. Subject of lecture, 'Ship's Routine'.

…ninety Military Police were detailed to effectively patrol the ship night and day.

The ship got underway at 8 p.m…

FRIDAY 30 June 1916

…At 2.30 p.m. a practice alarm was held… It was found that the ship's siren was not audible below deck D and a system of bugle posts was inaugurated throughout the ship to pick up the alarm. It was found in this and subsequent practices, that the bugles with the officers' and NCOs' [non-commissioned officers] whistles were sufficient to pass the alarm to all parts of the ship.

Four machine guns were mounted on A deck, fore and aft, with a competent and adequate detail to operate them under the command of two competent machine gun officers…

SATURDAY 1 July 1916

A practice alarm was held at 3p.m. and based upon previous experience, an officer was placed on the fore well deck and forecastle deck to hurry the men to A and B decks, to assure a steady flow of men.

On Friday, as well as today, full use was made of the swimming bath, units having travelled the farthest being detailed for its use first.

Lieutenant Norman Edgar Sharpe was on board. He had heard rumours that 'the Germans will get the *Olympic* this run. That ought to make the trip more interesting.' On their departure, he saw 'two or three men taken off as suspects.'[4] (The *Washington Post* reported: 'Two German spies carrying explosives were discovered on the British troop ship *Olympic*… the two men were brought ashore.' Another rumour circulated in June 1917. The *Manitoba Free Press* stated: 'Rumours of Canadian troops being lost in the supposed torpedoing of the big ship are as unfounded as the report that she had been sent down…') Whether there was any truth in the rumours or not, *Olympic* was fine. By Tuesday 4 July 1916 they were 'in the war zone at last. The ship zig zags from side to side, the decks slanting a bit on each turn.' Two destroyers appeared at 5 p.m. and *Olympic*, north of Ireland, 'quit zig zagging'. She arrived safely at Liverpool the following afternoon.

Following a refit early in 1917, she continued to sail generally between Liverpool and Halifax on the Canadian run; later in the war saw stops at New York, as well as Brest and Southampton, for she played her role in conveying American troops as well. In May 1918, she rammed and sank the *U103*, becoming the only passenger liner to sink a U-boat during the conflict. One lucky escape happened in the war's final months, in what appears to have been an attempted attack by Otto von Schrader's *U53* early on the morning of 4 September 1918.[5] One torpedo slammed into *Olympic*'s port side amidships and failed to explode; nonetheless, it pierced the outer plating and flooded part of the inner skin. The damage was not noted until she was dry-docked in February 1919. After the armistice, she ferried troops home to Halifax.

Olympic appears to have recently docked at New York on 12 October 1918. The 6in guns on the forecastle and well deck are visible; signal lamps have been fitted below the bridge wings; and a rangefinder was mounted on the roof of the bridge. (United States National Archives and Records Administration)

Above: The torpedo-shaped object visible in the fore well deck is a paravane or 'otter': one was streamed from the bow on each side of the ship, while in dangerous waters, to offer protection against moored mines. (United States National Archives and Records Administration)

Above: *Olympic* appears in a second version of her dazzle paint schemes (type 19, design AX). The chains on either side of the bow are associated with the minesweeping paravanes. (United States National Archives and Records Administration)

HALIFAX OCEAN TERMINALS. S.S. OLYMPIC. COALING. MARCH 28th 1919.

In August 1919, *Olympic* returned to Harland & Wolff for an extensive refit to make her ready for passenger service. Although other vessels enjoyed remarkable war records, ships such as *Aquitania*, *Leviathan* (the old *Vaterland*) and *Mauretania* were laid up for extended periods, whereas *Olympic*'s service was particularly hard. She was in service, essentially, from September 1915 onwards, except for the required overhauls. Hers was a remarkable war effort and she enjoyed a special acknowledgement when IMM's annual report for 1918 was issued. It referred: 'to the exceptional war services rendered by the White Star Line SS *Olympic*, the largest British steamer.' As well as carrying 201,040 persons[6] 'without one life being lost', she had 'steamed 184,000 miles, consuming 347,000 tons of coal, without the slightest delay of any kind or accident to her machinery, a record which is probably unique in the history of shipping.'

Notes

1   Vickers, James. 'The *Britannic* Sinking', *Titanic Commutator*, 1977, p.17.

2   'Part Four: The Final Journey of the *Britannic*…', *Titanic Commutator*, 1991, vol.15, pp.19–24. The officer's diary gives a very personal account of the sinking and is believed to have been written by Fielding. It refers to all of the other officers except the second and fifth, and was donated by great-grandson Richard Kirk.

3   Hayes, Captain Bertram Fox, *Hull Down* (Cassell & Co.: 1925) p.194.

4   My thanks to Mary Anne Sharpe for her time, and sharing her father's wartime diary.

5   See my article: 'Target *Olympic*: Feure!' *Titanic Commutator*, 2008, vol.32, no.184: pp.161–65.

6   'Report of the International Mercantile Marine Company for the Fiscal Year Ended 31 December 1918.' Office of the International Mercantile Marine Co., 51 Newark Street, Hoboken, NJ (New Jersey), 2 June 1919. The figure was also given by the White Star Line in a post-war brochure for *Olympic*; J.H. Isherwood's figures, published in *Sea Breezes* in 1956, gave a total of 200,857. These figures are practically the same whereas some much lower estimates are incorrect.

Below: A splendid view of *Olympic* coaling at Halifax and giving a wide perspective of the ocean terminals, taken on 28 March 1919. (From the collection of the Maritime Museum of the Atlantic)

THE ROARING TWENTIES

BACK ON TRACK

When *Olympic* left Southampton on 25 June 1920, nine years to the month since she had entered service, the *Southampton Times*' reporter felt she looked 'even better than when she made her first voyage'. She had been the first of the large liners to be converted from coal: the boilers were now fuelled by oil instead. Her performance was all that had been hoped for, while the change made refuelling considerably easier and quicker. The paper reported she had 2,249 passengers on board and her westbound bookings were very strong throughout 1920. On one crossing she carried 2,403 passengers. Many people were keen to go to America.

Unfortunately, the White Star Line were hindered by the lack of a suitable running mate. They improvised a service with *Adriatic* on a temporary basis, but she was slower than *Olympic*. To make matters worse, the United States tightened immigration restrictions in 1921. The figures show the stark decline: in six months in 1920, *Olympic* carried a total of 8,609 third-class passengers westbound – an average of 1,076 on each crossing; by 1923, she was carrying only 4,512 – an average of 322. The American restrictions were tightened further in 1924, by which time all the major pre-war liners had returned to service to compete for passengers.

By the summer of 1922, White Star had finally achieved the cherished ambition of a large three-ship express service from Southampton to New York. They were able to acquire some of the tonnage surrendered by Germany: *Columbus* (renamed *Homeric*), and *Bismarck* (renamed *Majestic*).

Soon dubbed 'The Magnificent Trio', alongside *Olympic* they were to maintain a regular schedule for the next ten years. Cunard's *Mauretania*, *Aquitania* and *Berengaria* competed directly with the White Star ships, and they now sailed from Southampton as well. The increasing competition, combined with far fewer third-class passengers, caused *Olympic*'s passenger lists to decline from her record of almost 38,000 passengers in 1921. As was to be expected, she was more popular than *Mauretania* (her chief rival when she entered service), while newer ships such as *Aquitania* and her running mate *Majestic* in turn had an edge over her. Nonetheless, *Olympic* remained one of the most popular express liners afloat after 1924, carrying around 25,000 passengers every year until the end of the 1920s.

Her enduring first-class passenger lists showed the wisdom of the White Star Line's focus on comfort. She carried her share of celebrities, from Mary Pickford, Douglas Fairbanks and Charlie Chaplin in 1921 to Arthur Conan Doyle in 1923, the Prince of Wales in 1924 and J.B. Priestley in 1931. She was called the 'film star liner' in press reports, while the Prince of Wales' trip was well documented. When he was shown his 'parlour suite' on C-deck, he remarked that the Regence-style sitting room was 'too grand for me'. Captain Howarth incurred the company's displeasure when he allowed the Prince on the bridge while in pilotage waters.

Plenty of others enjoyed sailing on *Olympic*, not only the famous. Forty-seven-year-old Sidney Hackney was among the 1,225 passengers on the

One of many departures from Southampton in the mid-1920s. Of *Olympic*'s 257 round trips to New York, 215 took place after the war. (Author's collection)

Olympic at Southampton around 1922. She commanded attention and dominated the docks. (Günter Bäbler/ Mark Chirnside collection)

Left: An interesting view of *Olympic*'s bridge seen in this still image from a White Star Line publicity film, 1921. (Author's collection)

Right: Arthur Conan Doyle, his wife Jean and their children Denis, Adrian and Billie, standing at the forward end of the promenade deck, A, on 2 April 1923. The crow's nest is visible in the background. Arthur Conan Doyle had also been a passenger in 1914, after which he wrote a description of *Olympic*'s appearance as he imagined her at sea:

No sailor could fail to recognise that glorious monarch of the sea, with her four cream funnels tipped with black, her huge black sides, her red bilges, and her high white top hamper, roaring up channel at 23 knots and carrying her 45,000 tons as lightly as if she were a five-ton motor boat. It was the queenly *Olympic* of the White Star Line – once the largest and still the comeliest of liners. What a picture she made with the blue Cornish sea creaming round her giant forefoot, and the pink western sky with one evening star forming the background of her noble lines!

(Arthur Conan Doyle collection – Lancelyn Green Bequest, Portsmouth City Council, ACD1/B/1/20/52)

return leg of *Olympic*'s last round trip of 1927. He was impressed by the ship's food and luxurious furnishings, not to mention the 'magnificent staircases and fireplaces'. In the midst of the 'flapper era', his daughter remembers still that her father was surprised at the dancing on board. 'To watch the "flappers" with their short skirts, silk stockings, long ropes of beads, bobbed hair, rouged lips, long cigarette holders and cocktails, dancing… must have been quite something,' she writes. Sidney's daughter still remembers going to meet her father on his return, at Waterloo: 'We had a hired car and a chauffeur to drive us to the station from our home in South London and my mother and two elder sisters were all excited by his homecoming. I can see him now, a tall good looking man… in a handsome checked overcoat, carrying a large beribboned basket of exotic fruits surrounded by suitcases, people and porters.'

Passengers on *Olympic* had not chosen the fastest liner afloat, but there was always an interest in the ship's performance. In July 1922, it was reported that she had reached and maintained 27.82 knots for several hours, a remarkable but highly dubious claim. On one occasion in August 1923, claims of a race between *Olympic* and *Leviathan* led to White Star Line officials issuing a denial. In fact, *Olympic*'s average speed had been slower than usual on that particular crossing, but *Olympic* did better her American rival the following summer. On 5 July 1924, she left New York on the same day as *Leviathan*. Although the American ship scored a clear victory in terms of carrying a higher passenger list, the White Star ship put up a remarkable performance. It took her five days, twenty-two hours and forty-seven minutes to cover 3,241 miles at an average speed of 22.7 knots. She was not driven at full speed, although one day's run was a record 550 miles: extremely good for an eastbound crossing. There was no doubt that *Leviathan*'s average speed came in at a lower 22.65 knots, but she covered fewer miles, which meant that her voyage time was faster than *Olympic*'s even though her average speed was lower.

Occasionally, *Olympic*'s speed led to some very good luck for anyone betting on the length of the day's run. In August 1925, two of the 668 first-class passengers had an eventful voyage to New York. Harry G. Martin had been promised that a friend would forward him sufficient funds for his tickets, but after he had boarded at Cherbourg without a ticket his friend changed his mind. He was in luck when his father was able to send a cheque for $338.30, enabling him to fund his ticket to his home city of New York. John McKeon was extremely lucky, for he won a lot of money. He bet $500 that the ship's run would be either above 535 miles or below 525 miles, and when it came in at 523 miles his gamble paid off. He won $2,000 from betting on the day's run on two occasions. He won even more participating in card games in the smoke room.

★

Collisions and other accidents were a fact of life. In March 1924, *Fort St George* collided with *Olympic* while she was backing out of her pier at New York, resulting in serious damage to the White Star liner's stern frame. *Fort St George*'s commander was held responsible. On 16 September 1926, *Olympic* went to the aid of the damaged steamer *Ellenia* in mid ocean and stood by to assist. There was some confusion as to whether her commander wanted to abandon ship but, after discovering that he wanted to be towed, Captain Marshall decided *Olympic* could assist no further. Another approaching vessel, *Laguna*, would do the job.

Fog, storms and general poor weather conditions often caused frustration and disrupted the express liners' schedules. The North Atlantic was one of the most hostile of the world's oceans. She encountered a severe storm during an eastbound crossing in December 1921. In *A Journey to India*, first-class passenger Albert Bemis recalled:

About nine o'clock Monday morning a great comber struck the ship just forward of the main saloon. I was taking my bath at the time, on the lee side, and felt it strike but thought little of it. The wave broke through all the portholes of the music room [reception room] and flooded the room and a part of the dining saloon and put six or eight inches of water in the cabins on the deck below. Splashing upward on the side of the ship, it tore away a piece of steel railing two hundred feet long, not to mention the after-housing of one of the lifeboats on the boat deck, probably seventy feet above the *waterline* [original emphasis]. Fortunately, only a few passengers were about at the time…

Several of the Marconi wires were severed, leaving them whipping around dangerously from the masts for several hours. When lunch was finishing that day, *Olympic* gave several quick rolls and dislodged a number of items of furniture. 'She behaved splendidly all through, except for the rolling,' Captain Hayes remarked. Unfortunately there was more than just damage to the ship. One third-class passenger died when he fell and fractured his spine, while another had to have one of his legs amputated after a watertight door slammed closed and crushed it.

When *Olympic* arrived in New York on 20 December 1922, she was fifteen hours late after running into a blizzard and gales of 75 miles an hour. Among the ship's 581 first-class passengers was one lady who took such a dislike to the weather that she wrote a letter to the captain, suggesting that he tie 'the ship up somewhere until the sea became calm again'! Not only were the ship's masts and superstructure covered with snow and ice, but several portholes on D and E-deck had been smashed by the heavy seas. At one point during the crossing, the ship was slowed to 'half speed ahead' since the snow 'made it impossible for the officers on the bridge or the lookout man in the crow's nest to see further than a ship's length ahead.'

On 30 September 1924, *Olympic* and her 1,160 passengers reached the Ambrose Channel lightship, only for the weather to frustrate any hopes for a timely arrival. For several minutes, Captain Frank Howarth and the pilot felt that 'it would be better to anchor' until the fog cleared and the weather improved:

Olympic was within a quarter of a mile of the Gedney buoy in the channel at 4 o'clock when the captain saw that there would not be room for the big ship to make the turn and [*Olympic*] had to back out down toward the lightship again. The *Olympic* was drawing thirty-four feet and there was only forty feet of water in the channel. Her three big propellers churned up a quantity of mud when the engines were put full speed astern, which caused many of the first class passengers who were looking over the rail to imagine that the liner had struck the west bank of the Ambrose Channel and had gone aground.

The morning before *Olympic* arrived in New York on 16 June 1925 was rather dramatic. Already, she had slowed down on two occasions because of fog, which lost about five hours. At 3.20 a.m., about an hour before she passed the Nantucket Lightship, 'a thunderbolt dropped into the sea ahead of the ship with a terrific report and lightning flashed like the lash of a whip across the heavens', according to one reporter's account. They stated that the lightning 'zigzagged across the sky and lit up the horizon like day.' Less than a month later, *Olympic* was fifteen hours late getting into New York. One day, over a twelve-hour period from 6 a.m. to 6 p.m., the fog had been so thick that the forecastle deck was hardly visible from the bridge. Consuelo Vanderbilt, wearing 'a yellow silk frock with a black hat', had cause for astonishment when one of her friends greeted her at the foot of the gangway. Her friend was wearing precisely the same outfit!

An unfortunate coincidence, perhaps, for Consuelo turned to her mother: 'Her frock is the same as mine, and they told me in Paris that mine was the only one of its kind.' It was some consolation that they both had the same good taste.

Even the tide in the North River, while *Olympic* was docked at Pier 59, could cause difficulties. On 5 August 1925, as passengers were beginning to disembark and walk down the gangways, the 'strong flood tide' caught the stern 'with such force that the bow rope parted with a loud report and the ship slid back about twelve feet. The movement was slow, and the officers had time to rush the passengers off the gangways and lower the bridge to the pier again.' No one was hurt and a number of tugs had to be employed to move *Olympic* back.

When *Olympic* arrived in New York on 21 November 1928 – carrying J.P. Morgan junior, as well as 316 other first-class passengers – severe storms had delayed her by no less than sixteen hours. One account depicted the sea's fury:

…seas came over the bow with such force that they tore away thirty-five feet of the iron railing on the forecastle deck, tore off an iron door, and swept the full length of the promenade deck. Windows were smashed on the starboard side of the promenade deck.

Captain W.H. Parker described the seas as mountainous. One threw him off his feet and he had to crawl up to windward on his hands and knees to regain his footing.

A 'blinding snowfall' slowed *Olympic* down when she left New York at noon on 28 December 1930. It 'blanketed everything from the view of the captain and the pilot on the bridge', forcing her to proceed slowly until she passed Quarantine an hour later. One man who was sad to see *Olympic* leave was Ben Fidd, who had been searching on board the liner for his pet lizard. The lizard, which he had cherished for ten years, had apparently been frightened by some cats and was thought to have stowed away on *Olympic*. Fidd hoped that one of the deck stewards would find him and bring him back to New York on the next crossing.

Challenging weather conditions and other difficulties were an inevitable part the North Atlantic run, yet changing circumstances arose as the 1920s drew to a close.

★

Sarah Leeds enjoyed her trip to Paris, crossing eastbound from New York to Cherbourg on board *Olympic*. After dinner in New York with family, she and her companion Ruth were on deck to watch their departure at 1 a.m.: 'a small boat followed us quite a distance up the river displaying fireworks'. The next morning, Saturday 5 July 1924, they found time to unpack and arrange the 'beautiful flowers' in their first-class stateroom. 'I just adore it on shipboard and our living in a continuous thrill,' she wrote.

They met 'two attractive young men' on deck the next day and 'the four of us played bridge after dinner and walked the deck'. Paul and Bob ('bright eyes' and 'little sunshine' respectively) came from Pittsburgh and 'turned out to be excellent dance partners … they are so adorable'. She walked on deck with Paul. Perhaps he was the person who told her that *Olympic* had just completed 550 miles – a record for an eastbound day, which was shorter than a westbound one because the clocks were put forward; and accomplished with an average speed closer to 24 than 23 knots.

On Tuesday, 'Paul and I defeated Ruth and Bob most severely – they had to bow to our superiority – and then the game [of quoits] ended.' Then on the next day 'after dinner Ruth and I were asked to take up the collection for the orchestra which they say is quite an honour as the prettiest girls onboard are always chosen… Paul and Bob were on hand but we dismissed them as they were "tight" and consequently met some very attractive people.' By Thursday, they spent much of the morning getting packed and, after an evening's dancing and champagne, they were 'landed at Cherbourg at 7 a.m. after being transported from SS *Olympic* on a tender'. Although there had been rough seas, she enjoyed the crossing.

'It was a 6 hour ride from Cherbourg to Paris. Bob and Paul were with us all day – and were adorable. I never shall forget that ride. Paul called us up at the hotel (Edouard VII) tonight and we went to the Chateau Madrid for dinner and dance with a friend of the Dennison's. It was a perfect reproduction of paradise.'

From left to right, Paul, Sarah, Ruth and Bob pose on the port side boat deck outside the grand staircase. (Author's collection)

Sarah relaxes in a deckchair on the promenade deck's after end. The entrance to the veranda café can be seen behind her. (Author's collection)

A Marconigram informs Sarah's father that she is having a pleasant voyage. (Author's collection)

SECOND-CLASS TRAVEL
IN JULY 1925

Twenty-six-year-old Harold Osborn travelled eastbound on *Olympic* in 1925. He was an Olympic athlete who set a record for the decathlon at the games in Paris in 1924. During his voyage, he wrote a series of letters to his sweetheart. A few short extracts shed light on life at sea:

FRIDAY 10 JULY 1925
Our first day at sea has passed very quickly and inconspicuously, a wee bit of fog early in the forenoon and late afternoon. Our stewards awakened us at 7.30 a.m.. Breakfast about 8.30 a.m. then to the top deck to read, take pictures, play shuffle board and anything else we can think of. Lunch at 1.00 p.m. Then some more reading and a little work out. We got a medicine ball and tossed that around, skipped a rope, played leap-frog and what not. Got a good sweat up and then took a salt water bath. After that I mended some clothes, and here I am, writing until dinner time (See I need a wife.) The stewards are clearing the library now as if they may be preparing for a dance this evening. The first is ours!

SATURDAY 11 JULY 1925
We made 512 miles yesterday and by midnight probably 550 more, maybe 600 and then will be slightly more than a third of the way across.

We attract considerable attention when we work out, but I guess it is advertising the club. We passed two ships yesterday and one today. I only saw the first yesterday. Too lazy to look for the last two. Ah, yes at lunch, no at dinner last night we had white wine, two small cups each. It was really very good.

SUNDAY 12 JULY 1925
Took some pictures today and also one of a 'freighter' that we passed. I took the last from a porthole and got all over [illegible].

...I didn't dance last nite and tonite [sic] being Sunday I believe there is none. Some of the boys have been dressing up and going over to first class. They report it very easy to get by...

...So far none of our bunch has had the slightest touch of seasickness, although, I believe that some of the passengers have. This evening the ship is rolling much more than usual and I imagine it – the ocean –

Left: 'Shuttleboard [sic] SS *Olympic*' in July 1925. From left to right, Harold Osborn, an unidentified companion, Roy Dodge and Herb Swartz enjoy a game of shuffleboard. (Susan Osborn Jones collection)

Right: 'Shirley Jobann SS *Olympic*'. A young girl poses for a photograph in fine sunny weather on *Olympic*'s second-class boat deck promenade. The raised section behind her is the roof of the first-class smoke room, where shuffleboard was played. Although deck chairs were not generally used on the first-class section of the boat deck prior to the war, the second-class deck had an abundance. (Susan Osborn Jones collection)

gets a wee bit rougher, there will be more of us that will be hunting a secluded spot.

He commented that there were not many young people in second class.

MONDAY 13 JULY 1925
Another lazy day has passed into oblivion. Days at sea are very much the same. One gets so that they do the same things at the same time, and almost in the same way.

Yesterday being Sunday, instead of dancing, we had a concert from the ship's orchestra… They played it much better than they do dance

music. They are too stiff and 'sort' of old fashioned. Almost like a German one, perhaps it is their English stolidity showing up.

…I really haven't told you a thing about our ship, quarters, meals, or anything so I'll proceed to do so without further delay. The good ship *Olympic* is the fourth largest in the world…Has over 11 decks or stories. Our bunch has three staterooms. Three of us are in the same I'm in. The largest and the smallest, 290 and 135. all of them are outside staterooms, that is they have a porthole. That makes them much cooler and nicer for sleeping. We have room for four, two regular berths and a sort of settee that serves as a bed. This settee alas has a back which can be lifted up for the [stops suddenly] They are of course more nicely furnished than third [class] and the beds are softer otherwise there isn't much difference. One can be just as lonesome in second as third, depends on the person. However, nice people, boys and girls, do go second rather than third, our dining room seats about 300 I suppose, finished in light oak and red tables and chairs. We eight have a nice round table, all to ourselves, and the best waiter of the lot. Each stateroom has a steward and when one wishes to take a bath, the bathroom steward gets everything all ready. I'm afraid I'll be more spoiled than I am.

…For our meals we have usually five courses, hors d'oeuvre, fish, meat, pudding, ice cream, it was good quality…

WEDNESDAY 15 JULY 1925
Not another day left. That certainly is good news to a land sick person. Our voyage, tho' hasn't seemed long.

I was finished just after the gong was sounded, just before I got in the chair we met the *Leviathan*, second largest ship in the world. Tonite sometime we meet the *Majestic*, the largest, and one of this company's own line. We met a large freighter or passenger vessel last nite [sic], according to reports. I didn't see it, however, as I wasn't on deck.

…Then two school teachers that Paul – not me – had gotten acquainted with came around and asked us to make a tour of the ship with them. In charge of one of the stewards we went all thru [sic] first, second and third class. Saw the engines, kitchen and all. it was quite interesting, and I was glad I got to go. The boat is certainly fixed up nice in first class, like a nice – very nice – hotel.

We got our landing cards today. We reach Cherbourg, France tomorrow morning at six. We are supposed to see the 'toe' of the English boot at about eight… Cherbourg was where we landed last summer, when on the Olympic trip. Then we are supposed to dock at Southampton at 2.30 p.m.

RISE OF THE TOURIST TRAVELLER

After the decline in immigration, the 'tourist' passenger came into being in 1924. As they explained in the early 1930s: 'the White Star Line inaugurated on some of its ships a new class of travel called "tourist". It was solely for the use of educated tourists desiring to travel economically yet in solid comfort. In an amazingly short time it became an institution with Americans…'

Olympic brought her first 'tourist third cabin' passengers to America when she arrived in New York on 5 August 1925, carrying a mere eighty-nine of them among her 1,095 passengers. Only 497 tourist third cabin tickets were sold for *Olympic* towards the end of 1925, and all westbound. Tourist third cabin passengers were allocated either the most attractive third-class accommodation, or the least attractive second-class staterooms, at a reasonable price. Although the new class proved increasingly popular on board *Homeric* and *Majestic* (they carried 18,245 tourist third cabin passengers between them in 1926 and 1927), the White Star Line did not offer any tourist third cabin tickets again for *Olympic* until 1928, which was perhaps something of a missed opportunity.

When the tourist third cabin tickets were first sold in 1925, these passengers did not even have their own public rooms, and that problem was remedied when *Olympic* underwent her annual overhaul at Southampton in December 1927 and January 1928. Many improvements were introduced. In first class, a new dance floor was installed in the lounge, the Café Parisien was redecorated and several additional staterooms were fitted on A and B-deck with their own private bathrooms. Second class was refurbished throughout. Tourist third cabin now had their own dining saloon, lounge and smoke room, while third class had: 'A big, new, airy lounge; a spacious new smoke room; a newly arranged dining saloon, all pleasantly-furnished, attractive places where the passengers can gather in great comfort.' The new public rooms for tourist third cabin and third-class passengers were created in several ways. A new bulkhead ('to be soundproof, but with hinged ventilating window flaps at top') was installed, partitioning the original second-class dining saloon. The starboard side remained available to second-class passengers, while the smaller port side served as the new tourist third cabin dining saloon; some of the original second-class staterooms on the port side were removed to make way for another tourist third cabin dining area immediately aft. The third-class general room and smoke room, beneath the poop deck, had been refurbished and were allocated to tourist third cabin. A new third-class smoke room and general room were created, taking up the original third-class area forward on D-deck. Given the decline in third-class travel, these public rooms were ample.

The overhaul and refit preceded a successful year for *Olympic* in 1928. She carried over 26,000 passengers, which was her best showing for six years; and her average passenger lists rose steadily from 1926 to 1929. In September 1928, Captain Walter Parker took over command from Captain William Marshall, who had been promoted to the larger *Majestic*. After inspecting *Olympic* together, Marshall seemed sad to be leaving his old ship. Since Parker had been transferred from *Homeric*, he did not have a preference for either

Left: Passengers relax on deck. (Author's collection)

Above: This photograph from a White Star Line brochure depicted *Olympic*'s forward grand staircase: 'Here, as in other parts of this beautiful ship, panelling and carvings in oak lend a tone of substantial dignity.' Although posed, it is easy to imagine first-class passengers in formal dress descending the staircase to the reception room, prior to dinner. (Author's collection)

Above: 'Pure white walls and ceiling and abundant light from large windows give this large room a cheerful air.' The image's caption neglected to mention a key feature of the dining saloon: out of view at the side, the leaded glass windows had strips of Linolite directly behind them, illuminated at night to give the effect of daylight; in daytime, the Luxfer prismatic panes, situated between the windows and the outer portholes, were intended to disperse the light evenly so the portholes' outlines were not visible. (See p.82) (Author's collection)

Above left: After dinner, men in first class ascended to the smoke room at the aft end of A-deck: 'polished mahogany walls inlaid with mother-of-pearl make this room a symbol of ornate ship construction.' (Author's collection)

Above right: A lady in first-class stateroom C90 (originally designated as C84 in 1911). The stateroom was in Adam style with pure white panelling and doors, whereas the Adam-style adaptation for the 'parlour suite' sitting room employed mahogany doors. (Author's collection)

and offered to take *Majestic*. Marshall responded: 'I suppose I ought to feel honoured. She is, after all, the largest ship in the world, you know, Parker – but I am leaving the *best* [original emphasis] to you, for all that.' And so, Parker took over *Olympic*: 'Such a magnificent command.'[1] Lord and Lady Kylsant were among the passengers returning to Britain in November 1928. They took a keen interest in the ship and made notes for improvements, which were carried out when *Olympic* returned to Southampton at the end of the year to undergo her annual overhaul.

Two thousand workmen were working continuously for four weeks. The first-class dining saloon was enlarged slightly at the expense of the reception room, while 'a new specially polished parquet floor' was laid in the centre; more two- and four-seat tables were installed in light of passenger demands; and it was refurbished throughout. Another dance floor was installed in the Café Parisien. Meanwhile, the barber's shop off the after grand staircase on C-deck was 'completely rebuilt' and a ladies' hairdresser added. *Olympic*'s first-class lounge and second-class library were also fitted with cinematography apparatus ('fitted with a safety control minimising possibility of fire'), although silent films were shown and 'talkies' would not follow until 1931. Although more than fifty private bathrooms were

Above: Christopher Morley, writer of the *New York Evening Post*'s 'Bowling Green' column, visited *Olympic* in 1922. He showed a particular interest in the first- and second-class literature. The library steward in first class said that 'ninety percent' of passengers wanted detective stories; his second-class counterpart said love stories were 'most in demand'. (Author's collection)

Right: A view of the second-class dining saloon in 1921. In the post-war period the original long tables were replaced with more intimate, smaller tables. (Daniel Klistorner collection)

Left: *Olympic*'s orchestra plays for the passengers dancing outside the lounge in the second-class entrance aft on C-deck. (Daniel Klistorner collection)

Below: A stylish advert depicted *Olympic*'s profile in the late 1920s. Even after the White Star Line reverted to British ownership in 1927, IMM was retained as its agent in the United States. (Author's collection)

THE BACKGROUND OF MODERNITY

Our present modern life wouldn't be so vibrantly brilliant without the background of Europe. European art and culture make the woof of its sophisticated fabric ▬▪▪▬ And it's just as essential in the background of a private life ▬▪▪▬ When you go, travel correctly — on either a White Star, Red Star or Atlantic Transport liner. That is a fitting entree — mingling with men and women of the world — people you enjoy knowing ▬▪▪▬ Being identified with their social and sports life on board is fascinating in itself.

WHITE STAR LINE
RED STAR LINE · ATLANTIC TRANSPORT LINE
INTERNATIONAL MERCANTILE MARINE COMPANY

No. 1 BROADWAY, NEW YORK, OUR OFFICES ELSEWHERE OR AUTHORIZED AGENTS

added, undoubtedly the most significant change was forward on B-deck. The original staterooms were removed and the accommodation extended out to the ship's side, sacrificing the promenade deck, to make room for sixteen new large staterooms ('all equipped with private bathrooms, and with their roomy wardrobes they are really self-contained suites') decorated in a range of styles. 'The entrances and companionways have been re-decorated in handsome oak panelling with a new treatment giving the appearance of corridors in an old country house,' explained *White Star Magazine*.

Right: In her final moments and increasingly unmanageable, *Britannic*'s bow submerged as her list to starboard increased. Moments later, the engines would be stopped for good. Her loss in 1916 deprived the White Star Line of a useful running mate for *Olympic* after the war. *Britannic*'s absense was keenly felt in the 1920s. (Painting © Stuart Williamson, 2006/Author's collection)

S.S. "BRITANNIC"
RED CROSS HOSPITAL SHIP
SUNK BY GERMANS WITHOUT WARNING NOV 29TH 1916
50 LIVES LOST

Left: An interesting glass painting of *Britannic*. Aside from numerous inaccuracies in the depiction of the ship, the date and number of lives lost were incorrect. (Author's collection)

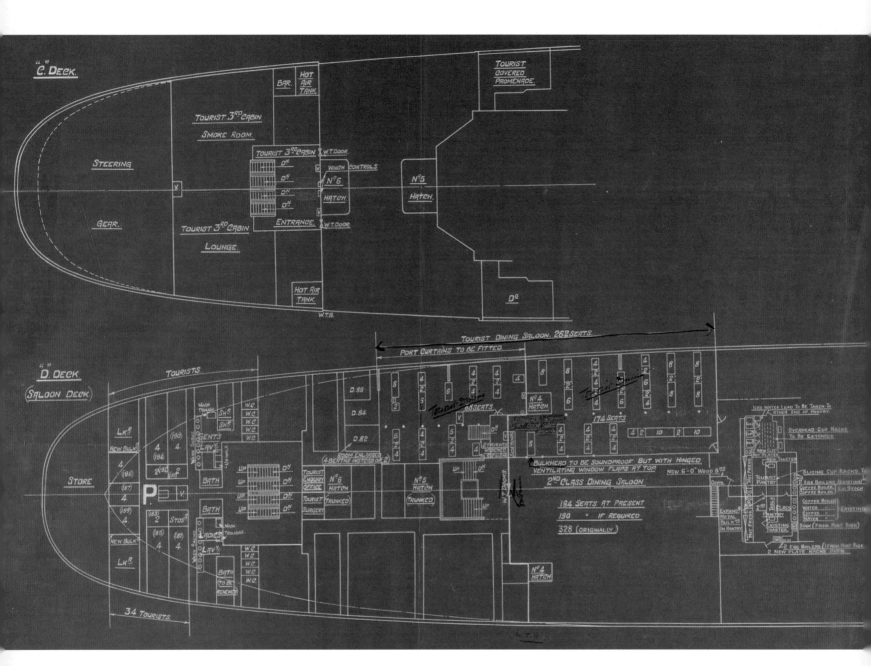

A plan showing the White Star Line's proposals to partition the original second-class dining saloon, create tourist third cabin dining areas, and improve *Olympic*'s galley equipment during the 1927–28 overhaul. The proposed tourist enquiry office and surgery can be seen aft on D-deck. (National Archives, United Kingdom)

CHIEF ENGINEER JOHN HERBERT THEARLE

Many of *Olympic*'s crew developed a fond affection for her, serving on board for many years.

John Herbert Thearle was born in Liverpool in 1869. Educated at the Liverpool Institute and Western School, Bath, he served his apprenticeship at the David Rollo engineering works on the Mersey between 1885 and 1890. He joined the Dominion Line in March 1899, before being appointed second engineer on *Republic* in 1903, after the IMM combine had been formed. By the end of the decade, he was serving on board the prestigious *Oceanic*.

He joined *Olympic* at Belfast in mid March 1911, serving as second engineer before he was promoted to senior second engineer in August 1911. He stood by the ship at Belfast on 11 October 1912, after she had arrived for her first major refit, and consequently missed his son Laurence's birth three days later. He remained with the ship for years and steadily climbed the ladder of promotion: in November 1915, he was temporarily appointed chief engineer; in January 1916, he was assistant chief engineer; and after serving alternately as chief and assistant chief engineer, by April 1919 he was appointed permanently as *Olympic*'s chief engineer.

During the ship's annual inspections, her boiler rooms and machinery spaces were always distinctly clean and well cared for – a sign of the pride that the ship's engineering staff took in their work. In the summer of 1921, Andrew Fletcher, President of the American Locomotive Company, was shown around the ship's engine room and saw the enormous reciprocating engines. He wrote to Thearle: 'I have not forgotten the splendid condition and shape the engine and boiler room was in, and have taken pleasure in stating the fact to a number of my steamship friends.' Another visitor spoke of the 'high standard of cleanliness and proper upkeep'.

Certainly, the ship's engineering staff had to have an authoritative command. According to one apocryphal account, one officer who was introduced to Thearle told him: 'I believe that I knew your father and a more murderous old Turk never sailed the high seas.'

Thearle only left *Olympic* once he had reached the White Star Line's compulsory age limit, leaving the ship at the end of 1929 and retiring officially on 1 January 1930. Captain Walker Parker retired as well. *Olympic* was dubbed the 'orphaned' *Olympic* by one reporter who noted that she had lost both her captain and chief engineer. It was estimated that Thearle had covered 1.6 million miles during his eighteen years caring for *Olympic*'s propulsion system.

His successor, Charles William McKimm, had also served on board since 1911, and he remained right through until 1935. When *Olympic* went to the scrap yard, he lamented:

She has been my home for twenty-four years, and I am sad to think that I have to say goodbye now. How is she going? The *Olympic* is going today better than ever. We had her engines reconditioned three years ago and since then she has been like a new ship.

It is almost sacrilege to destroy her after the performance she put up on this last voyage from Southampton. I could have understood the necessity if the 'Old Lady' had lost her efficiency, but the engines are as sound as they ever were. Better, in fact, than when they were first installed in 1911.

A wonderful photograph taken several months after the war's end shows *Olympic*'s engineering officers on deck while she was at Halifax. Assistant Chief Engineer Thearle (seated third from right) retained a copy that was signed by Captain Hayes (seated fourth from right). (Nick Thearle collection)

Olympic appears on a White Star Line sailing list in March 1926. (Author's collection)

A stylish depiction of *Olympic*, with her size exaggerated even further and the tug boat appearing tiny in comparison. To the left, the Statue of Liberty can be seen behind her, and the three-funnel liner heading in the opposite direction is surely her running mate *Majestic*. (Author's collection)

Olympic returned to Halifax for the first time since the war. In 1931, she made two cruises from New York to Halifax and back (6 August 1931 to 10 August 1931 and 27 August 1931 to 31 August 1931). She also undertook a Thanksgiving cruise from 25 to 28 November 1931 as well as completing sixteen round trips to New York. She did not undertake as many cruises as other vessels – *Mauretania* was largely used for cruising after 1931 and *Homeric* from 1932 – but they represented an effort by the White Star Line to try to earn additional revenues during the Depression years. The large building in front of the ship's second and third funnels still stands today and is the Nova Scotian Hotel. (Ioannis Georgiou collection)

A second-class passenger list from June 1928. The focus is on her passengers, exiting from an enormous White Star, but the four-funnelled silhouette is unmistakable. *Olympic* enjoyed a successful year with the highest total number of passengers carried since 1922. (Author's collection)

Above left: A colour depiction of an Empire-style stateroom. 'The bedrooms in these suites are designed to suit those accustomed to luxury and good taste in their homes; they are both dignified and comfortable, fitted with beds finely fashioned in rare woods or brass, with box springs and stuffed hair mattresses. To this add the finest linen and downy blankets; such are the bedrooms that ensure to the passenger that deep and refreshing sleep which is an essential part of the voyage.' Part of C-deck's starboard 'parlour' suite, the Regence-style sitting room is visible through the open door. (See p.139) (Author's collection)

Above: The first-class smoke room, 'a room of rich effect; instantly attractive by the handsomeness of the mahogany panelling, carved in fine detail; by the simplicity of the moulded white ceiling which gives full value to the rich mahogany of walls and beams. Here in this room, which combines the dignity of a club with the intimate comfort of a room at home, the passenger settles in the well-cushioned chairs, content just to live and enjoy life.' The first-class smoke room floor was changed after the war. (Author's collection)

Left: 'The Veranda Café is deservedly one of the most popular parts of the *Olympic*. Situated aft of the smoking room it looks right out across the illimitable ocean, stretching in the sunshine or deep blue under the stars… Light refreshments can be obtained here at all times.' (Author's collection)

Above: Two staterooms in Tudor were included in the sixteen large staterooms fitted at the forward end of B-deck in 1929. This one appears to be stateroom A23, the smaller of the two Tudor rooms, situated on the starboard side off the grand staircase. The letter is 'A' rather than 'B' following a change to the ship's deck designations at the start of 1929. (Author's collection)

Right: An advertisement for *Olympic*'s two weekend cruises in 1932. Although first- and tourist-class tickets were sold, all public rooms were available: 'The first class restaurant and Café Parisien will be available for *á la carte* meals, snacks, refreshments, tea and supper dances at moderate charges. Deck games, swimming galas, dances, talkie cinema shows, bridge and whist drives, every form of entertainment is provided and the energetic passenger can sample all in the three days the cruise lasts… the finest weekend holiday of your life.' (Author's collection)

**TO EUROPE
OLYMPIC
NEW TOURIST CLASS**

The entire former Second
Cabin accommodations—
all staterooms, public apart-
ments and decks—have now
become Tourist Class on the
Olympic.

WHITE·STAR·LINE

Left: The cover for a 1932 brochure advertises *Olympic*'s new tourist accommodation. After the end of 1931, the tourist third- and second-class accommodation was merged and branded as the 'new tourist class'. (Author's collection)

ABSTRACT OF LOG.

Triple-Screw R.M.S. "OLYMPIC" 46,439 Tons.

Commander : J. W. BINKS, R.D. (Lieut.-Commander R.N.R., Retired.)

CRUISE AROUND THE SCILLY ISLANDS VIA CHERBOURG.

Took departure from Nab Tower at 2.54 p.m. (B.S.T.) 30th July 1932.
Position at noon July 31st latitude 50.16 north, longitude 05.42 west
" " " August 1st " 50.26 " " 01.28 "
Arrive Nab Tower 2.30. p.m. August 1st. (B.S.T.)

Above: A rare souvenir Abstract of Log for *Olympic*'s 'cruise around the Scilly Islands via Cherbourg'. It was her second cruise in 1932. Unlike those for her normal Atlantic crossings, each day's run is not given, nor is the total time elapsed or the average speed. To satisfy that curiosity, after taking a short detention into account she steamed for one day, twenty-three hours and thirteen minutes, covering 574 miles at an average speed of just over 12 knots. The cruises were not numbered as her regular round voyages were and so the cruise was simply voyage '220a'. (Author's collection)

This page and next three pages: Accommodation plans showing the tourist accommodation. White Star advised tourist passengers that they would 'live in a charming, democratic atmosphere without sacrificing any of the comforts and reasonable luxuries of modern ocean travel'. (Author's collection)

DECK **A**

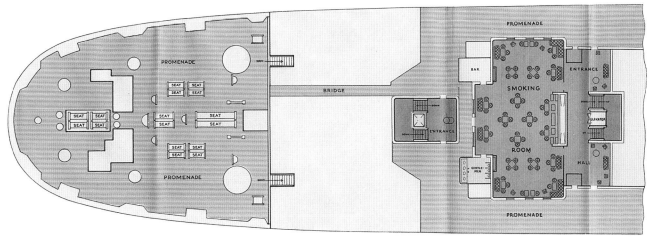

DECK **B**

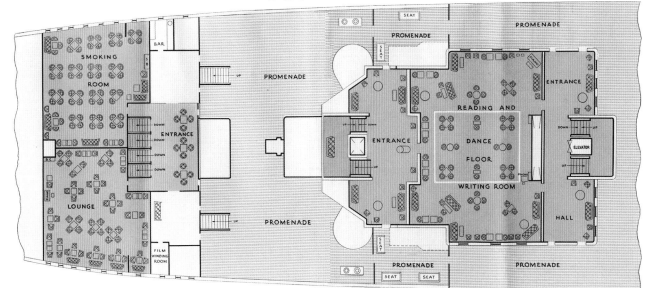

DECK C

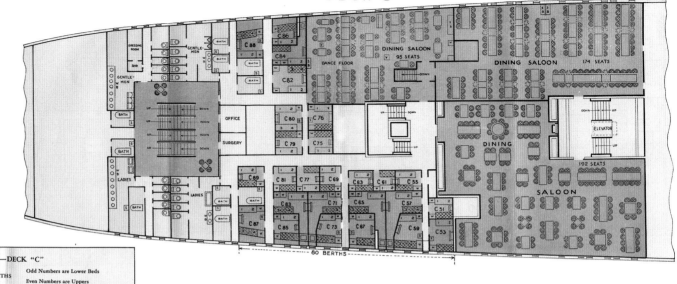

INDEX—DECK "C"

SUITES AND ROOMS WITH PRIVATE BATHS	Odd Numbers are Lower Beds
	Even Numbers are Uppers
OUTSIDE ROOMS	W. Indicates Wardrobe
INSIDE ROOMS	Indicates Wash-Basin
	Indicates Settee
BATHS AND LAVATORIES	S. Indicates Folding Seat

DECK D

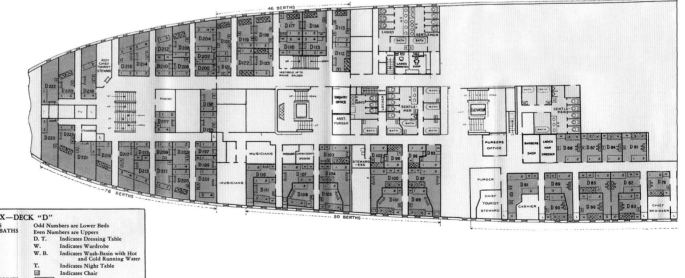

INDEX—DECK "D"

SUITES AND ROOMS WITH PRIVATE BATHS	Odd Numbers are Lower Beds
	Even Numbers are Uppers
	D. T. Indicates Dressing Table
OUTSIDE ROOMS	W. Indicates Wardrobe
	W. B. Indicates Wash-Basin with Hot and Cold Running Water
INSIDE ROOMS	T. Indicates Night Table
	Indicates Chair
	Indicates Settee
BATHS AND LAVATORIES	D. Indicates Chest of Drawers
	S. Indicates Folding Seat

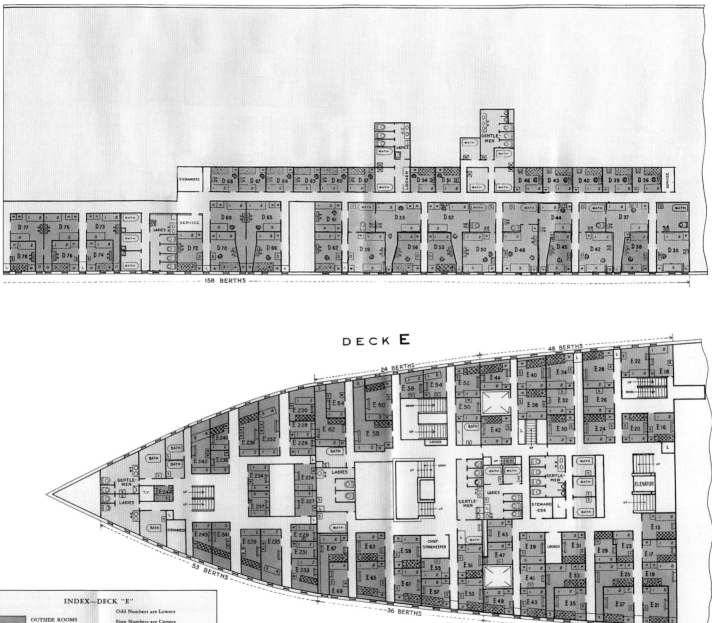

DECK D

DECK E

158 BERTHS

48 BERTHS
24 BERTHS
53 BERTHS
36 BERTHS
54 BERTHS

INDEX—DECK "E"

Odd Numbers are Lowers
Even Numbers are Uppers

OUTSIDE ROOMS

INSIDE ROOMS

BATHS AND LAVATORIES

I̲   Indicates Wash-Basin
W.   Indicates Wardrobe
S.   Indicates Folding Seat
     Indicates Settee

DECK F

III BERTHS

INDEX—DECK "F"

Odd Numbers are Lowers
Even Numbers are Uppers

OUTSIDE ROOMS	▯ Indicates Wash-Basin
INSIDE ROOMS	W. Indicates Wardrobe
	S. Indicates Folding Seat
BATHS AND LAVATORIES	⣿ Indicates Settee

Right: The dance floor in *Olympic*'s original second-class library, now known as the reading and writing room; and a tourist stateroom that was formerly first class, complete with features such as hot and cold running water. (Author's collection)

Left: The original third-class general room, redecorated and improved for tourist third cabin, became part of the combined tourist accommodation. (Author's collection)

Below: *Mauretania* in Southampton's floating dry dock. *Olympic's* funnels can be seen in the background, where she is docked, in this fascinating image from November 1928. (© Clifton R. Adams/National Geographic Society/Corbis)

Above: *Olympic*'s four funnels inside the White Star are unmistakable. (Author's collection)

Below: A mail sticker for *Olympic* from the early 1930s. (Author's collection)

FAMOUS BRITISH SHIPS

OLYMPIC

Above: *Olympic* appears on a cigarette card. The way she is illustrated hints at the times: her bow appears similar to that of the new motor ship *Britannic*, which entered service in 1930. (Author's collection)

Right: *Olympic* was featured on the *White Star Magazine*'s front cover for over a decade. The magazine was in its final year of publication when this issue was published in September 1933. Although she was surpassed in size by *Majestic* in 1922, and newer ships joined the fleet, she remained a sentimental favourite. (Author's collection)

N° 121
6D

SEPTEMBER
1933

WHITE ★ STAR
MAGAZINE

The Sea, Ships, Ocean Travel
and
THE ORGAN OF THE WHITE STAR LINE

This page and next three pages: *Olympic's*
first class accommodation plans, dating from
June 1934, were one of the last that White Star
published before the merger with Cunard. Many
changes had taken place over the years, including
the smallest details such as the installation of a
cocktail bar in the Café Parisien in 1931. The
number of private bathrooms quadrupled from
forty-two in 1911 to 168 in 1929, so that about
two-thirds of first-class passengers could access
these facilities, without accounting for some
private bathrooms in tourist. It is something
of a myth that the lack of private bathrooms
condemned the older liners to the scrap yard;
by the 1930s, passenger numbers were so much
lower that any first-class passenger who wanted a
private bathroom could secure one. The first-class
staterooms forward on the original D-deck (now
C-deck) had been reallocated to tourist class by
January 1935. (Author's collection)

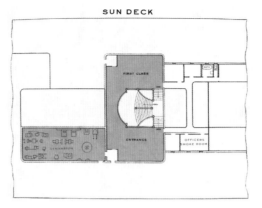

SUN DECK

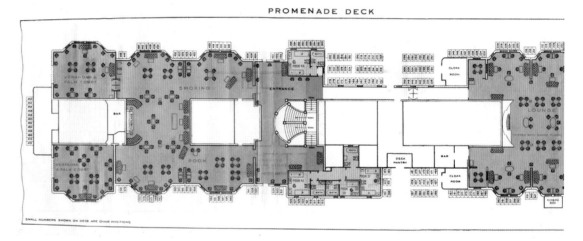

PROMENADE DECK

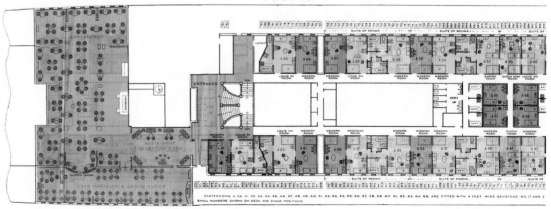

DECK A

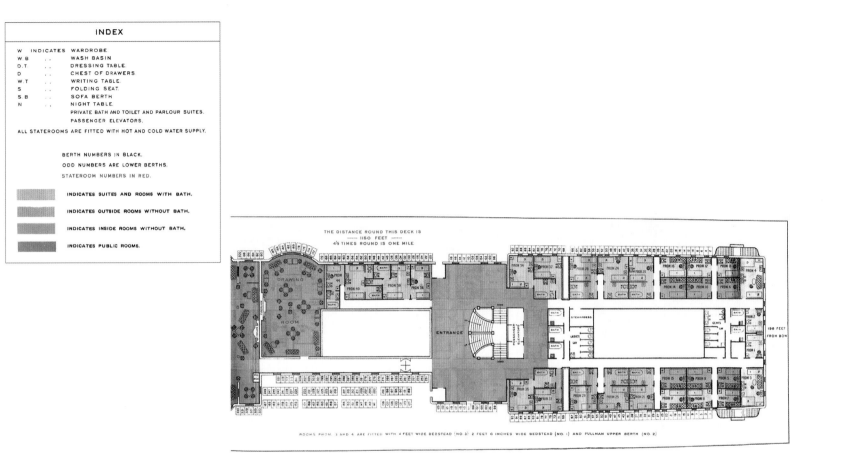

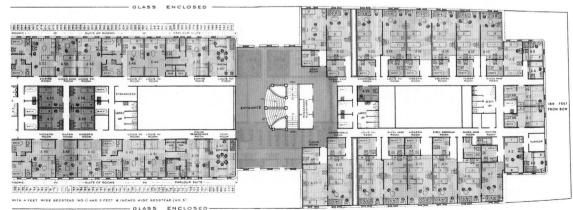

DECK B

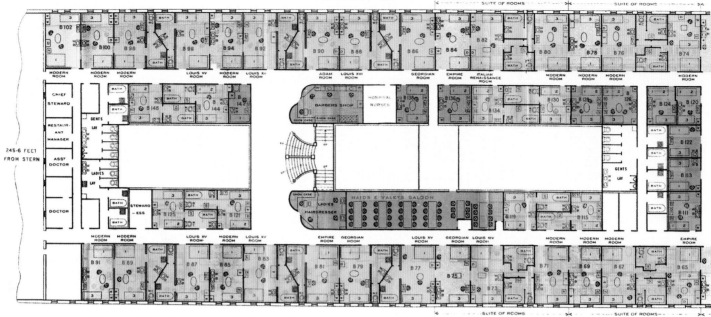

STATEROOMS B 55, 57, 59, 61, 63, 64, 65, 66, 67, 68, 69, 70, 71, 72, 73, 74, 75, 76, 77, 78, 79, 80, 81, 82, 83, 84, 85, 86, 87, 88, 89, 90, 91, 92, 94, 96, 98, 100, 102, ARE FITTED WITH 4 FEET WIDE BEDSTEAD
THE PORTHOLES ON DECK B ARE

DECK E

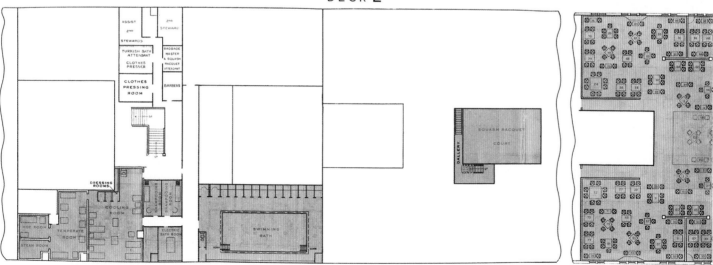

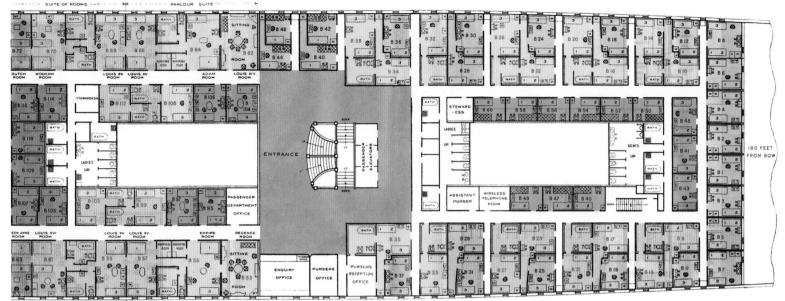

DECK C

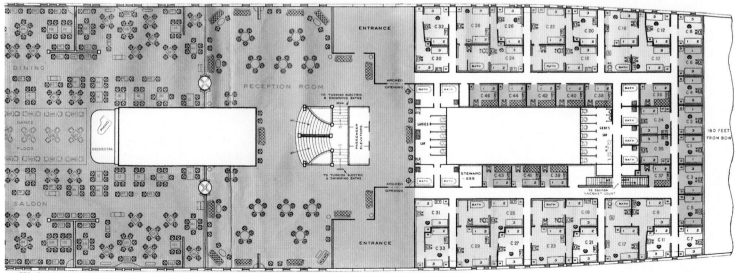

OLYMPIC TOURIST CLASS

THERE'S an undeniable thrill in crossing the Atlantic in a ship as large and magnificent as the Olympic. Her very dimensions are impressive . . . 882½ feet long . . . 92½ feet broad . . . her gross registered tonnage, 46,439 . . . and 52,000 tons displacement.

But the appeal of the Olympic's Tourist Class is not measured solely in terms of bulk . . . nor in terms of steadiness or speed, qualities which the Olympic nevertheless possesses to an extraordinary degree. Everything about her and in her is of regal dignity and quiet elegance . . . and you will experience too the warm satisfaction of being served by a staff literally bred in the highest standards of British stewardship and courtesy . . . trained for generations in smoothing your way . . . anticipating your needs . . . making your voyage a thoroughly comfortable and happy travel experience.

Your lounge is a vast salon of quiet distinction, recalling the charm of England's baronial mansions . . . easy chairs grouped about tables for bridge or chess . . . comfortable divans . . . a large bookcase filled with modern and classic literature.

A gleaming dance floor and an excellent orchestra invite you to try your newest dance steps.

In the smoking room english oak has been used with fine artistic effect in producing a room of dignity and simplicity, while deep, sturdy leather chairs and other fittings provide that complete relaxation so necessary to masculine comfort.

To the bright, cheerful dining saloon you will bring an enormous appetite whetted by sea breezes. Tables seating four, six, or eight persons, and covered with gleaming silver, shining crystal and snow-white napery, present a scene as animated as it is beautiful at mealtimes.

Then, when you retire to your charming, well-ventilated stateroom each evening, you will realize that you sleep as well as move in gracious surroundings aboard the Olympic.

Left: *Olympic*'s collision with the Nantucket Lightship (see p.153). (Painting by Charles Mazoujian, United States Coast Guard collection)

Above: An interesting advertisement for *Olympic*'s tourist accommodation, in a brochure that was published several days after she had completed her final round trip in April 1935. The top right photograph shows the tourist-class dining saloon. In December 1933, *Olympic* completed a brief overhaul, during which her tourist dining saloon 'received special attention'. The new décor was very 'modern': 'pink and grey form the new colour scheme for the whole room, the colours having been chosen... after copious medical tests regarding the effect of colours on the digestive system! Two hundred new chairs were fitted in this room, and more separate tables arranged for parties of four.' Following the merger of the second and tourist third cabin, the larger second-class section became tourist class and the smaller tourist third saloon, still in sober oak, became third class and retained its fixed swivel chairs. (Author's collection)

One of the two spiral staircases inside *Britannic*'s bow at F-deck level, leading down to the firemen's tunnel. The tunnel enabled them to access the boiler rooms from their quarters. Not long after the explosion, the tunnel was already flooding. (© Leigh Bishop)

On the starboard side of *Titanic*, aft of the navigating room at the rear right-hand corner of the wheelhouse, Captain Smith's accommodation comprised of a large sitting room, bedroom and private bathroom. A full carpet was provided in the commander's sitting room on *Olympic*, leading Thomas Andrews to note that the linoleum tiles would be unnecessary on *Titanic*. By 1996, the roof of the deckhouse was giving way and the bulkheads were angling outwards, exposing the captain's bedroom (to the right) and his bathroom (to the left). Today, the bulkheads lie completely flat on the boat deck and the roof over Fourth Officer Boxhall's stateroom (to the far left) is collapsing. The officers' quarters deckhouse and the superstructure more generally were lightly constructed compared to the structural hull beneath, making them more vulnerable to their hostile environment. To make matters worse, they are highly exposed to undersea currents on the topmost deck. (Courtesy © 1987–2010 RMS *Titanic*, Inc., a subsidiary of Premier Exhibitions, Inc.)

In 1993, an examination of *Titanic*'s interior revealed hints of its former grandeur. Originally fitted to the ceiling of one of the first-class grand staircase landings, this perfectly preserved first-class light fixture was now dangling by its wiring. This light fixture was probably photographed on A-deck: the light uses strands of crystal beads (seen on the boat and A-deck levels), rather than crystal bowl shades (seen on the decks below). (Courtesy © 1987–2010 RMS *Titanic*, Inc., a subsidiary of Premier Exhibitions, Inc.)

The port side of *Titanic*'s forward expansion joint, which intersected the officers' quarters deckhouse behind the bridge, photographed in 1996. The deckhouse forward of the expansion joint (on the left of the picture) shows deformation and damage compared to the deckhouse on the right-hand side. The left-hand window belongs to first-class stateroom X (one of a small number of staterooms at this level); the middle one belongs to a lavatory and the right-hand one to a bathroom. It is interesting to note that the expansion joint is open much wider than it would ever have been in normal service. When the bow impacted with the ocean floor, the decks towards the aft end of the bow section collapsed downwards; it appears the bow's enormous momentum caused compressed water to blow out the starboard hull plating beneath the well deck, the number 1 hatch cover was thrown hundreds of feet ahead of the wreck, and the wreck 'curved' somewhat, helping the expansion joint to open up beyond its design limits. (Courtesy © 1987–2010 RMS *Titanic*, Inc., a subsidiary of Premier Exhibitions, Inc.)

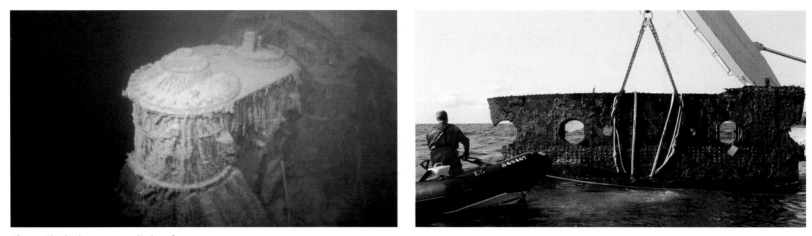

Above: The high-pressure cylinder of the starboard engine was photographed in 1996. *Titanic*'s stern section is in far worse condition than the bow. The main reciprocating engine room is wide open following the break up, revealing the enormous port and starboard engines. Debris from the upper decks can be seen resting on top of the engine. The foremost, low-pressure, cylinder and the forward part of the engine are no longer in place. (Courtesy © 1987–2010 RMS *Titanic*, Inc., a subsidiary of Premier Exhibitions, Inc.)

Above right: A significant section of *Titanic*'s hull, now known as the 'Big Piece', was recovered from the wreck site in 1998. It weighs 15 tons and is more than 26ft in length. The plating was originally from the starboard side of C-deck and it detached from the main body of the ship when the break-up occurred. The immense forces literally ripped through the steel. It formed part of the 'sheer strake' that was the side plating at the uppermost part of the structural hull. In this area of the hull, the rivets were hydraulically driven; the plating was doubled, heavily strapped and riveted for additional strength, so that the hull was several inches thick in places. (Courtesy © 1987–2010 RMS *Titanic*, Inc., a subsidiary of Premier Exhibitions, Inc.)

Panelling from *Olympic*'s first-class lounge is still in use today at the White Swan Hotel in Alnwick, Northumberland. When she was withdrawn from service, the hotel's then owner Algernon Smart, who had been a frequent passenger, bid for the first-class lounge's panelling and ceiling, which was then installed at the hotel. As a brochure put it in the early 1920s: '*Olympic*'s lounge is a magnificent salon, pronounced by many persons the finest room ever built into a ship.'

That *Olympic*'s lounge endures is a mark of its quality. When some of *Britannic*'s unused panelling and furniture was auctioned after the war, that panelling was described as 'almost exclusively solid mahogany and oak' that had 'been seasoning for a period of at least thirty to thirty-five years'. *Olympic*'s lounge is seen here, arranged as a theatre (left), and prepared beautifully for a wedding (above left and right). (Classic Lodges/White Swan Hotel)

Olympic's Café Parisien was refurbished over the winter of 1927–28. (Ray Lepien collection)

The new dance floor in the first-class saloon, 1929. (Ray Lepien collection)

Left: One of the new first-class staterooms forward on B-deck, which were ready when she made her first crossing in 1929. This one (A14) was described as Colonial in its style. Its numbering reflects the changes to *Olympic*'s decks during her refit in 1928–29, when A-deck was referred to as the promenade deck; B-deck became A-deck and the decks beneath were altered similarly. (Ray Lepien collection)

Below: The barber's shop was completely rebuilt in 1928–29. To the left can be seen the door leading to the first-class staterooms; on the right, the aft grand staircase. On the starboard side, a new ladies' hair dressers was fitted: 'Both these shops, painted an old apple green, have quaint bow-fronted windows in the eighteenth century style of St. James, in which are exhibited toilet articles and souvenirs for sale to passengers', advised the White Star Line in March 1929. (Ioannis Georgiou/Mark Chirnside/Daniel Klistorner/J. Kent Layton collection)

A postcard depicts *Olympic*'s running mate *Homeric* in the floating dry dock (above); and *Majestic* berthed at the 'Ocean Dock' (below). *Homeric* was withdrawn from North Atlantic service in 1932 and was employed on a number of cruises until 1935; *Majestic* was withdrawn from North Atlantic service in February 1936, and so the photographs were taken some years before the card was posted in July 1936. (Author's collection)

In March 1929, a month after her return to service, *Olympic* had the honour of hosting Admiral Jellicoe when he visited Southampton and 'was enrolled as a Freeman of the Borough'. On view in the first-class lounge, for 400 guests to see, was a letter from 3 November 1914 which Jellicoe had written, praising Captain Haddock's 'magnificent handling' of *Olympic* during the rescue of *Audacious*' crew. Following lunch in the dining saloon, Jellicoe added 'a word of deep appreciation of the fact that this hospitable occasion is taking place aboard such an historic ship as the White Star liner *Olympic*'. He recalled meeting Captain Hayes on board in 1918, as well as *Olympic*'s war experiences such as sinking *U103*. Although Haddock could not attend due to ill health, Hayes had come all the way from Liverpool.

Two months later, *Olympic* left Quarantine 'in the record time of eighteen minutes' before docking at 9.30 p.m., since 'health authorities followed their recent practice of accepting the word of the chief surgeon that there was no sickness onboard'. Tourist third cabin continued to be popular, while at the westbound season's height in August and September 1929, she carried 3,446 passengers to New York on two crossings. Her performance westbound was particularly good that year and saw the highest passenger lists since 1923. One passenger recounted his enjoyment of *Olympic*, in a letter published by IMM's *The Ocean Ferry* in January 1929:

> The Quaker Oats Company
> 17 Battery Place
>
> Managers, White Star Line: I had the pleasure – my wife accompanying me – of making a round voyage on the *Olympic*, and would like you to know that in all respects these ocean trips were the most pleasant and comfortable that we have ever taken. The food, service and atmosphere were beyond criticism – could not possibly have been better. I had often heard that the *Olympic* was in a class by herself – now I know it.
>
> W.A. Moran,
> New York Manager, Export Sales

Unfortunately, the White Star Line itself was encountering increasing difficulties. In January 1927, Lord Kylsant had purchased the company's shares from IMM, to be held by a new company, White Star Line Limited. The schedule of instalments stretched out to 1936. Part of the large and complex Royal Mail Group, Kylsant used his new company to expand his shipping empire with a series of extravagant and unnecessary purchases. He

S. S. LEVIATHAN & S. S. OLYMPIC
IN SOUTHAMPTON DOCKS

did so using the proceeds of the dividend payments from White Star's shares, but paying out a high share of profits to Kylsant hindered investment in the White Star fleet. In June 1928, the keel was laid at Harland & Wolff for a huge new liner, *Oceanic*, for the express service, but a lack of capital forced construction to be suspended the following year. The company's overdraft was increasing and, in 1929, two thirds of the somewhat disappointing profit went straight out again as shareholder dividend payments to Kylsant. His plans required a significant revival in shipping fortunes, at a time when they were already showing signs of decline. Following the Wall Street Crash in October 1929, his hopes evaporated into the bleak economic Depression.

Above: *Olympic* and *Leviathan* docked at Southampton in the late 1920s. (Author's collection)

Notes

1   Parker, Captain Walter H., *Leaves from an Unwritten Log Book* (Sampson Low, Marston & Co. Ltd: 1931) pp.264–65

A TIME OF HARDSHIP

YESTERDAY'S NEWS

Throughout the 1920s there had been relatively little challenge to the older liners, even though newer ships began to appear towards the end of the decade. When the new German liner *Bremen* wrested the Blue Riband from *Mauretania* in the summer of 1929, her triumph symbolised a newer generation. Not only was competition increasing; passenger numbers also began a catastrophic decline. The advent of newer ships posed a double problem as they took a larger share of a smaller number of passengers. In 1929, *Bremen* carried slightly fewer passengers than *Olympic*, but the German ship was only in service for half the year; in 1930, *Olympic* carried fewer than 20,000 passengers while *Bremen*'s total virtually doubled to almost 50,000. Her running mates, as well as the Cunard express ships, also showed dramatic declines in passenger numbers.

Berengaria carried an impressive 36,853 passengers in 1929, falling to 13,408 in 1931; meanwhile, *Mauretania*'s 16,922 passengers fell to 12,560; and *Olympic*'s 25,775 passengers in 1929 declined to 13,975 two years later. At the height of the season, she still had some good passenger lists, but the much smaller numbers that used to be seen only in the off season throughout the 1920s became much more frequent. When she left Cherbourg on 12 February 1931, her passengers included J.B. Priestley, who would go on to write the famous play *An Inspector Calls*. Set in early April 1912, it made reference to the 'absolutely unsinkable' *Titanic*. He found *Olympic* 'a friendly ship, for all her creaking,' writing a letter about his voyage:

The voyage has been pleasant enough although rather dull. On Tuesday [*recte* Thursday], getting out of the Channel, it was quite rough and many people were sick. I felt nothing then or since… After the sort of boats you and I are used to this ship hardly seems to move. She is very steady. The only thing is that she's noisier than a small ship – because you hear her expanding joints [sic] creaking and groaning all night. I've slept very poorly through late. The first three days I went up to the gymnasium before breakfast and began to feel very fit, since then I have had a touch of cold. Everybody has had a little. It's the quick changes of the Atlantic.[1]

Although the *New York Times* indicated that *Olympic* was delayed by fog, the ship's log also mentioned gales and 'very rough' to moderate seas. *Olympic* arrived on Tuesday evening, 17 February 1931.

One lady travelling in first class seems to have enjoyed her crossing. *Olympic* sailed from New York at midnight on Friday 27 May 1932 with 509 passengers: 129 first class, 218 tourist class and 162 third class. Although the sea was 'calm but cloudy most of the time, the only bad weather we have had was the fog Saturday forenoon, the fog-horn blew all the time until noon,' she wrote. She opted to eat in the dining saloon and tried to 'eat lightly' but found it 'rather hard when there is so much on the menu'. Her suite had 'room enough for six to sleep' with a private bath. She noted that there were more tourist-class than first-class passengers on board. She bought some match boxes for her nephew, while she remembered 'movies, dancing, [and] parties' during the voyage. On Monday 30 May 1932 there was 'a costume party' with dancing in the dining saloon and 'wine and liquor as free as water'. The following evening, there was a celebration banquet for a Jewish couple celebrating their tenth wedding anniversary which 'did not break up until well into the morning.' She planned to take *Olympic*'s 3 August 1932 sailing back to New York.

When *Olympic* arrived back at Southampton on 14 October 1932, it marked her final crossing of the year. The White Star Line had already scheduled work on the port engine's bedplates to take place during the annual overhaul, but circumstances forced them to bring it forward when cracks were found in crankshafts in both the port and starboard engines while they were undergoing a routine adjustment. They had hoped she would only miss one voyage, but the repairs took longer and many of *Olympic*'s 400 passengers were transferred to *Georgic*, the company's new motor ship sailing from Liverpool. Fortunately, the double bottom under the engines was 'very carefully examined' and 'except for a few defective rivets, was found in satisfactory condition'. Although the company did not want to spend an estimated £60,000 replacing the bedplates entirely, they did take the opportunity to make substantial repairs and improvements. As well as renewing the defective parts, additional balance weights were fitted,

while the bedplates were strengthened. It is interesting to note that Cuthbert Coulson Pounder, a master marine engine designer, was involved in the changes, for his work helped put Harland & Wolff at the forefront of building diesel motor ships.[2] After twelve hours of sea trials, 'everything went very satisfactorily,' and on completion of the work the performance of *Olympic*'s engines was never better.

While she was undergoing the overhaul, rumours circulated around Southampton that she was going to be withdrawn from service. One journal, *The Engineer*, commented on 'exaggerated reports' that had 'appeared in the non-technical press relating to the condition of the *Olympic*'s machinery' and briefly described the engine work: 'The work now arranged... will, it is confidently expected, put the machinery and the ship in a condition to render many years of further useful service in the fleet of the White Star Line.'

Even for winter, passenger numbers remained dire. When *Georgic* took over two of *Olympic*'s cancelled westbound crossings, scheduled for January and February 1933, the popular new motor ship was unable to muster more than 200 passengers. While she was out of service, missing five round trips to New York according to one published schedule, White Star took the opportunity to refurbish *Olympic*'s passenger accommodation. The *Ocean Ferry* pointed out:

> Chief among the many new features are the entire overhauling of the first class entrance halls and staircases and the modernisation of staterooms. The job of restoring the ship was handled by Ashby Tabb, of Heaton Tabb & Co., Ltd, of London...
>
> Great thought and care was given to the *Olympic*'s new dress, so as to preserve the spirit and tradition which has grown up around her. The first class staircases are superb in any guise, broad and dignified, and far beyond in magnificence any ship of recent years.
>
> ...Many ideas were considered before it was decided to build up on a background of soft Georgian green, a harmony of colour in quiet tones relieved with the rich bronze balustrade, some touches of gold in the more prominent carved cornices, leading up to a number of decorative panels of classical landscapes, which were specially painted and form points of interest in the design.
>
> Great care was given to these panels, and many sketches were prepared so that the scale and character of the whole would be preserved. The panels were painted onboard the ship because the artist felt that the atmosphere of the new surroundings would be best preserved if they were executed in the environment in which they were to appear.

Olympic seen in the Solent from the Prince's Green at Cowes on the Isle of Wight, inward bound to Southampton during the great annual yachting regatta that occurred during the first week of August. (David Hutchings collection)

Furniture and curtains have been renewed, and many new effects have been produced with rich pelmets and hangings. Among other improvements many of the first class staterooms have undergone a change and a lighter touch has been introduced in accordance with modern ideas.

With the *Majestic*, world's largest ship, the *Olympic* will maintain the White Star Line's express service from New York to Cherbourg and Southampton…

She was 'not merely a ship, but an institution'.[3] *Olympic* left Southampton on 1 March 1933. Her engines performed well as they were eased gradually back into service. The *New York Times* welcomed her 'looking like new': 'Old travellers found a relief from this brightening up by going to the lounge, where the oak is still uncovered by paint, and the smoking room with its old Spanish mahogany untouched.' Her cargo included 140 bars of silver valued at £10,000, which were consigned to the American Metal Company. The return crossing had her lowest-ever passenger list, 125 people, including a mere thirty-nine first-class passengers.

On 2 June 1933, the musician Duke Ellington and his orchestra boarded *Olympic* at New York. Ellington was reputed to have a fear of ocean travel,

On 11 August 1933, *Olympic* was photographed at Southampton. *Homeric* can be seen ahead of her. *Olympic* left for New York five days later and enjoyed one of her most successful round trips that year, generating revenues of nearly £38,000. (Author's collection)

attributed to *Titanic*'s loss when he was twelve. A.H. Lawrence described Ellington's state of mind in his biography, *Duke Ellington and His World*:

Ellington's anxiety was exacerbated when the steward informed him that the ship was steered by an automatic pilot! He asked everyone, 'How can an automatic pilot see an iceberg?' He relieved his anxiety by staying up all night drinking brandy, writing music, and pacing the deck miserably until daylight…[4]

Ellington's party travelled tourist class, but after giving a concert in the first-class dining saloon on the second evening out, they were given the run of the ship. One recalled the grand staircase: 'It was elegance, pure elegance. I can't describe it, you had to have been there to see and experience it.'[5]

Olympic set a record that month 'for the discharge of mail': the 7,244 bags of post were already sorted when she arrived off Quarantine one Tuesday evening. The bags were all unloaded into tenders in one hour and eight minutes, 'an average of 106 bags a minute.' Although she had never been intended to set records for speed, even after twenty years' service *Olympic* performed well. From 1927 to 1932 she averaged 21.7 knots all year round, above her designed service speed and with ample power in reserve. In March 1931, she covered 576 miles at an average speed of 23.2 knots during a westbound crossing; from July to September 1933 she averaged around 22 knots for three consecutive westbound crossings; in September 1933 she averaged 23.43 knots in the English Channel.

Olympic also marked a sad milestone. Due to the decline in third-class travel, the last time she carried a passenger list of more than 2,000 was in 1923; she did not carry more than 1,000 passengers after 1933, during the Depression. Her total of 9,170 passengers for the entire year made it her worst year in service by that measure. The year's end also marked the collapse of the White Star Line. It had reported a series of heavy losses: £379,069 in 1930, the first loss in its history; £450,777 in 1931; £152,045 in 1932, and then £353,552 in 1933, which dealt a blow to any hopes of sustaining the improvement.

Cunard had suspended construction of their new express liner in 1931, and the government saw an opportunity for a merger between the two rivals to create a single strong British company. In October 1932, Chancellor Neville Chamberlain asked Lord Weir to report confidentially on 'the trading and financial position of the British shipping companies carrying on mail and passenger services in the North Atlantic, with special reference to the New York – European berth.' He endorsed the economic benefits of Cunard's plan for an express service operated by two larger and faster liners, writing: 'The

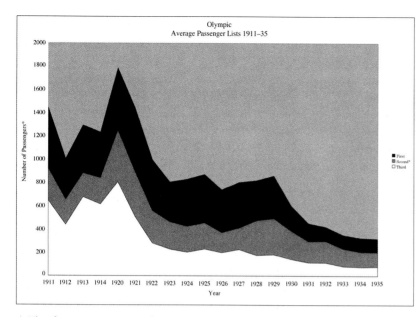

Olympic
Average Passenger Lists 1911–35

★ The figures are averages for one crossing, not one round trip, and cover both westbound and eastbound voyages. The totals for first, second and third have all been rounded, so the visible totals for all three classes should not be taken as precise figures. Second class includes the period when some tourist third tickets were sold in 1925, and *Olympic* was carrying both second-class and tourist-third-class passengers from February 1928 to October 1931: they are counted here as one total. After that time, her second- and tourist-third accommodation all became tourist class, and they are still counted as one total under the second class category.

Above: *Olympic's* commercial passenger carryings for each year she was in service help to give a general impression of the changing patterns in passenger traffic. While the chart does not reveal sufficient details to portray the specific changes from year to year, the broad trends – including the decline in third-class travel after the war and the dramatic decline in all three classes after the Wall Street Crash in 1929 and the subsequent Depression – are apparent. (Author's collection)

Right: *Olympic* can be seen entering Southampton's floating dry dock on 25 May 1934, when she was inspected for damages sustained during her collision with the Nantucket Lightship; fortunately, the damage sustained was fully repaired before the year's end. (Author's collection)

alternative form of investment in say three modern vessels of the "*Aquitania*" type would neither meet the competition nor yield the same economic return.'

Lord Essendon, White Star's chairman, was rather more sceptical of the 'big ship' policy, pondering a scaled-down fleet with three smaller ships operating from Southampton and the profitable new motor ships *Britannic* and *Georgic* out of Liverpool. The pair were 'undoubtedly the best paying ships of either' company's fleet, generating substantial profits. He had been encouraged by *Georgic's* performance when she substituted for *Olympic*, making a small profit despite so few passengers. Nevertheless, there was no realistic hope to save the White Star Line. Although Essendon disputed some of Weir's conclusions, wondering if he had 'started out with the preconceived idea' that Cunard was in a much sounder position, Weir pointed out that Cunard was meeting its financial obligations, whereas White Star was not. By 30 December 1933, the White Star Line's directors had agreed to the merger with Cunard. The government would provide financial assistance to complete the first new liner. Cunard White Star Limited was registered on 10 May 1934.

Above: Actress Elizabeth Bergner sailed on *Olympic* in January 1935. She is pictured on board, possibly sitting in the forward port side corner of the boat deck entrance to the first-class grand staircase. The settee cover is not commonly seen in *Olympic* photographs and was presumably a late addition, while the same can be said for the framed painting behind her. (Daniel Klistorner collection)

Olympic left Southampton the same day. Early on the morning of Tuesday 15 May 1934, she was proceeding in thick fog and was expected to arrive in New York around midnight. Her speed had been reduced several times, right down to 10 knots. *Olympic*'s officers believed that the Nantucket Lightship was just off the starboard bow and Captain Binks even ordered a course change of ten degrees as an extra precaution. Just after 11 a.m., the lightship was sighted directly ahead. Binks ordered the helm hard over, the port engine reversed and the watertight doors closed. *Olympic* began to turn and now the starboard engine was reversed as well: her speed fell to 8, then 6, then 4 knots…

It was too late. *Olympic*'s bow cut deep into the lightship's side, fatally wounding her. In his stateroom, first-class passenger Sir Arthur Steel-Maitland felt 'a slight jar'. Seven men were saved from the water by *Olympic*'s lifeboats, but three of them died subsequently. Sixty-five-year-old Captain Braithwaite of the lightship appeared frail, and smoked his first cigarette in fifteen years. The tragedy marked a return of some of the bad luck that she had had when she entered service. *Olympic*'s owners were faced with a lawsuit for $500,000 from the American government, reduced to $425,000 in July 1935 and then settled for $325,000 in January 1936.

END OF THE LINE

Cunard White Star's express service was maintained for the time being by *Aquitania*, *Berengaria*, *Majestic* and *Olympic*. Unfortunately, the passenger traffic did not justify the employment of so many ships. The company continued to try and reduce costs, including the closure of the *á la carte* restaurants on board *Olympic* and *Majestic* in October 1934, but all four ships were running at a loss overall. There were signs of improvement on the passenger front, but from a low level: early in 1935, *Olympic*'s passenger figures were up by about 40 per cent compared to the same period in 1934. In January 1935, the new company announced she would be withdrawn from Atlantic service; the following month, they discussed a number of improvements required for cruising. The plan was for *Olympic* to make a westbound crossing to New York, leaving on 29 June 1935. There would be a series of four or five cruises including destinations such as Quebec, Halifax and Bermuda, and *Olympic* would leave New York for Southampton on 28 September 1935. She would return to the express service with two further round trips to New York in November and December 1935, taking her to 1936 and her twenty-fifth year of service.

Following her arrival on 13 October 1935, *Olympic* lay at her wharf inside Thomas Ward's Palmer's yard. Her interiors were deserted until a private, then a public, viewing prior to auction. On 5 November 1935, Knight, Frank & Rutley began auctioning off *Olympic*'s fittings. These rare images show *Olympic*'s desolate public rooms: the grand staircase (below, top left) with the cherub, clock and other fittings removed; the first class lounge, bereft of furniture (below, top right), but with the large electrolier still in place (below, bottom left); a section of the lounge with fittings removed (below, bottom right); the fireplace in the first-class smoke room (opposite, top left); a number of electrical fittings (opposite, top right); several beds removed from the ship, including the left-hand one which was not original and a late addition by the 1930s (opposite, bottom left); and a section of panelling from second-class (opposite, bottom right).

The first-class lounge panelling survives today at the White Swan Hotel in Alnwick, Northumberland, and the large chandelier is at Cutlers' Hall, Sheffield, South Yorkshire. It is interesting to note that the painting above the smoke-room fireplace is Norman Wilkinson's *Approach to the New World*, which is now in Southampton's maritime museum alongside *Plymouth Harbour*, the painting used on *Titanic* and recreated for the museum by the artist's son. Surviving panelling from the *á la carte* restaurant is still afloat, having been used to furnish the cruise ship *Millennium*'s 'Olympic Restaurant'. (Joseph Carvalho collection, Titanic International Society Archives)

After lying at Southampton's Berth 108 all summer, *Olympic* made her final departure on 11 October 1935. Her paintwork shows signs of wear and tear and several of her lifeboats are missing on the port side. The thick cloud of black, oily smoke from the third funnel is a telltale sign of a ship that had lain idle for some months. Above the first funnel, the white cloud is probably steam dissipating from a long blast on the whistle, which served as a warning to other vessels that the ship was getting underway. (Author's collection)

Olympic's Captains

Name	Born	Certificate Number	Date
Edward John Smith	1850	14102	May 1911
Herbert James Haddock	1861	08765	March 1912
Harry William Dyke*	1871	023399	September 1915
Frank Ernest Beadnell	1871	023714	September 1915
Bertram Fox Hayes	1866	015917	September 1915
James Thompson**	1873	028224	March 1917
Bertram Fox Hayes	–	015917	April 1917
Alexander Elvin	1862	011031	January 1922
Sherwin Hambelton			
Hugh Frederick David	1866	019560	January 1923
William Marshall	1873	029116	September 1923
Frank Briscoe Howarth	1864	018043	November 1923
George Robert Metcalfe	1870	023469	January 1925
Eustace R. White	1873	026697	July 1927
William Marshall	–	029116	August 1927
Walter Henry Parker	1869	018514	September 1928
Eustace R. White	–	026697	August 1929
Walter Henry Parker	1869	018514	September 1929
Eustace R. White	–	026697	December 1929
George Ernest Warner	1870	025105	June 1930
Edgar Lukeman Trant	1874	028375	December 1930
John William Binks	1874	027112	December 1931
Reginald Vincent Peel	1875	031038	January 1935

Every effort has been made to be accurate. However, there are errors, contradictions and omissions even in primary source material such as crew agreements and a commander's own career papers.

* Harry William Dyke signed on as Olympic's master on 8 September 1915 at Belfast. He was superseded by Bertram Fox Hayes three days later, according to the log.
   Another entry in the ship's log states that Frank Ernest Beadnell, as master, had been superseded by Bertram Fox Hayes.
** James Thompson was listed as Olympic's commander in the ship's log, at Greenock in March 1917. His own papers had an entry that he was in command of Olympic at 5 April 1917, but it is known that Bertram Fox Hayes' proposed appointment to Adriatic was cancelled and he took Olympic instead.
   Alexander Elvin Sherwin Hambelton was recorded as the ship's commander at the same time as Thompson. However, it was merely an entry in a list of captains that survived in the Cunard archives. It is not confirmed by his own papers or Olympic's log.

Olympic completed her 257th round trip, leaving New York on 5 April 1935 and arriving at Southampton seven days later. Sadly, on Sunday 14 April 1935 – twenty-three years after *Titanic*'s loss – it was announced that the cruise schedule had been cancelled. It appears the company did not believe the cruises would be sufficiently profitable, particularly when combined with Atlantic crossings where they expected *Olympic* to register a loss. Cunard White Star had no further employment in sight for her. There were discussions that summer between various parties, including one consortium who wanted to purchase *Olympic* for use as a floating hotel in the south of France, but she was destined for the scrapyard when Sir John Jarvis purchased her. As a member of parliament, he planned to have her broken up at Jarrow, where she would provide a source of jobs for many of his unemployed constituents. The purchase price was £97,500. She left Southampton for the final time on 11 October 1935.

Her demise prompted a number of comments. Captain James Thompson, Cunard White Star's assistant marine superintendent, was quoted on 5 August 1935: 'The *Olympic* is the best ship that Harland & Wolff ever turned out of their famous yard at Belfast... She is in "A1" condition and can maintain 22½ knots under ordinary weather conditions if she has the fuel. I should be very sorry to hear of her going to the ship breakers.' When *Majestic* was withdrawn in February 1936 'veterans in North Atlantic shipping said that after the scrapping of the *Olympic*, recognised as one of the finest steamships afloat, there were no surprises left.' *Olympic* had remained seaworthy; her engines continued to perform well. Although interior decoration had moved on, other improvements had done much to improve passenger comfort. Two thirds of first class had private bathroom facilities and even a significant number in tourist class. *Olympic*'s withdrawal from service was the consequence of harsh economic reality during the Depression of the 1930s. Technology had advanced considerably: *Queen Mary* entered service in May 1936 and her sister ship *Queen Elizabeth* would follow. Cunard White Star were forced to withdraw *Berengaria* from service two years later, as her wiring deteriorated and the cost of making her seaworthy became prohibitive. Only *Aquitania* survived past the end of the decade; and that was because she was needed for government service after the outbreak of the Second World War.

Olympic passed into history. Workers from Thomas Ward's noted her hull was 'surprisingly sound'. By August 1936, her superstructure had been dismantled; in September 1937 she was towed to Inverkeithing for final demolition; and in February 1939 she was removed from the British register. Captain Hayes, who was in command for six years, described her as 'the finest ship in my estimation that has ever been built, or ever will be.'

Notes

1   Brome, Vincent, *J.B. Priestley*, (Hamish Hamilton Ltd: 1988), pp.109–11.
2   I am indebted to Scott Andrews for his advice on technical matters although, as always, all errors are entirely my own.
3   Daniel Klistorner deserves a specific vote of thanks for sharing such an interesting article.
4   Lawrence, A. H., *Duke Ellington and His World* (Routledge: 2003), p.159.
5   *Ibid.*

THE OCEAN'S SECRETS

Britannic's wreck was located by an expedition led by Jacques Cousteau in December 1975. He returned the following year to explore the vessel. Despite rumours that *Titanic* had been located in the 1970s, her discovery was announced publicly by an American–French team led by Dr Robert Ballard of Woods Hole Oceanographic Institution and Jean-Louis Michel of IFREMER in September 1985. Numerous expeditions have taken place to explore both shipwrecks.

BRITANNIC

The sinking of *Britannic* was simply one of many during the war. Perhaps that made her less interesting to some, but there were plenty of questionable allegations surrounding her loss. The discovery of her wreck provided the opportunity to assess some of those questions, with full-scale expeditions taking place in 1976, 1995, 1997, 1998, 1999, 2003, 2006, 2008 and 2009 to date. The site was described following a side scan sonar survey in September 2007:

> *Britannic* rests on her starboard side. The resulting sonographs seem to confirm that the wreck lies on a heading of 253° and on her side at an approximate angle of 85°. The tip of the bow sits slightly more upright than the other part of the hull of the ship… The first 40 metres of the bow, which bore the

brunt of the collision on hitting the bottom, are heavily twisted and contorted. However, sonographs show that the hull still remains in one piece.

> The 253° heading of the wreck seems to indicate that during the last half hour, the ship sailed in the opposite direction from which it was approaching prior to the explosion. The course of the ship during the sinking may have been affected by two factors: (i) the list to starboard which initiated a wide turn to the right; and (ii) the intensity of the currents in the area with prevailing currents flowing south-southwest. Sonographs show that the original superstructure of the ship, including deckhouses, mast, cargo cranes, giant lifeboat davits and Welin type davits, remains in remarkably good condition.[1]

Britannic had originally been steaming in a north-easterly direction, prior to the explosion. Captain Bartlett's intended course, when he tried to beach her, was to the south-east. She now lies pointing to the west-south-west. There is no logical reason whatsoever for him to have resumed steaming *away* from land; in the ship's final moments she was simply incapable of manoeuvring, and turned around when she was out of control.

Allegations that she was carrying troops or war weapons are without foundation. From surviving contemporary evidence, the British authorities placed a priority on the safety of hospital ships and did not want their role called into question. There was debate regarding the carrying of medical personnel as passengers, only on the previous voyage. No evidence has been found of any arms being carried and no cargo was declared lost. The forward cargo area that has been observed appears to be entirely empty. Nor is there

Right: Thirty lives were lost in *Britannic*'s sinking: nine from the Royal Army Medical Corps and twenty-one from the ship's crew. There are four graves – seen here – at Piraeus Municipal Cemetery at Drapestona, which are well maintained (Private Arthur Binks, RAMC, Fireman Joseph Brown, Seaman George Honeycott and Trimmer Charles Phillips). Spencer Genn, one of *Britannic*'s stewards, was injured during the sinking and admitted to the Russian Hospital at Piraeus. He died aged twenty-seven on 9 May 1917 and is buried in Ford Park Cemetery in Devon. The grave of RAMC Sergeant William Sharpe can be found at the New British Cemetery in Ermoupoli, on the Greek island of Syra (Siros). Unfortunately, his remains had been misidentified as 'Corporal Stephens' and the efforts of a number of people, including researchers Michail Michailakis and Simon Mills, led to arrangements being made to rectify the error in 2009.

Most of the victims were not recovered. Eight names (all from the RAMC and including, mistakenly, Sergeant William Sharpe) are listed on the Mikra Memorial in the Mikra British Cemetery, south of Thessaloniki, and a further eighteen on the Tower Hill Memorial in London. (Michail Michailakis collection)

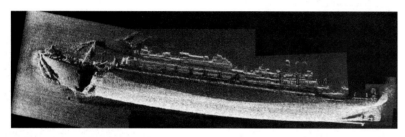

Left: *Britannic* as she lies today, seen through a composite image of three side-scan sonar images. When the ship came into contact with the sea floor, the forecastle and much of the bow crumpled in on itself, with the mass of the rest of the enormous ship behind it. Although other vessels of the period which lie on their side, such as *Lusitania*, have lost much of their breadth, *Britannic* appears to retain her full width and shape. There is no hint of any sort of collapse. The hull is completely intact save for the damage and split at the bow. (© Bill Smith)

any evidence that a coal dust explosion took place. Although it has been suggested, the conditions for such an explosion have to be quite specific, and the hatch above the reserve coal bunker hold is intact. It is interesting to note that the wreck's position was recorded on Admiralty charts over 6 miles to the south-west, leading to some suspicions that the authorities had not wanted the wreck explored. In fact, she turned out to be where Captain Bartlett reported in 1916, and an unfortunate error in her recorded position is hardly proof of anything untoward.

The damage to the wreck, where the bow is crumpled forward and then split open beneath the fore well deck, can be accounted for by the way in which the ship settled on the bottom. When he explored the ship in 1976, Jacques Cousteau believed that some of the hull plates were bent *outwards*, indicating a secondary internal explosion. However, through all the exploration that has taken place to date, the likelihood is that the answer was far simpler. By 2003, evidence had also been found of a number of mine bases with their anchor chains still attached, where German records indicated they had been laid and precisely where *Britannic* was heading that fateful morning. During that year's expedition, diver Richard Stevenson entered

boiler room 6 through the open watertight doors at the end of the firemen's tunnel. He believed that the next watertight door, leading to boiler room 5, was partially closed, but despite his efforts and those of Richie Kohler and John Chatterton three years later, it was not possible to access or film it. Although the starboard side of the ship is hidden, the observed damage and open watertight doors, combined with a number of visible open portholes on the port side, leave little doubt that they were enough to sink the ship.

Britannic's superstructure 'in general is in amazingly good condition considering its years underwater', reported 2003 expedition leader Carl Spencer. 'There is very little marine growth internally, however externally the superstructure is covered in mussels and hard fauna which is helping preserve the steel structure.' Unfortunately, debris had hindered an attempt to penetrate the main engine room, but diver Zaid Al-Obaidi observed one of the crankshafts and a connecting rod of one of the reciprocating engines. Spencer was impressed by 'the fact that the wreck is so intact in beautiful crystal clear warm water. *Britannic* was a beautiful ship and in many ways she is even more beautiful now with all of the colourful marine growth on her… The wreck is in exceptional condition…'[2] As Nick Hope, who dived in 1998, explained:

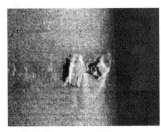

Left: Two of *Britannic*'s funnels lie near each other on the seafloor. They are still recognisable, although they have lost much of their original shape and are largely flattened. (© Bill Smith)

Below: A diver drops down to examine the poop, beneath the shade deck, at the very stern of the ship. The railing and other deck fixtures are visible, while marine growth covers much of the ship's deckhouses. (© Leigh Bishop)

Below left: Diver Richard Stevenson's examination of *Britannic*'s propellers helps to demonstrate the awesome size of the sunken ship. The port side propeller in the distance was responsible for many of the casualties of the sinking. It is now, forever, motionless. (© Leigh Bishop)

Britannic is simply the most awe-inspiring wreck that any of the team had ever dived... telegraphs hang by their chains on the captain's bridge, together with a helm. Just behind these the telemotor still stands perpendicular to the deck on the remains of the patterned linoleum that covered the deck in this area. And nearby we found a bath in the officer's quarters, toilets, and all sorts of other artefacts.

All indications are *Britannic* will remain highly preserved for years to come.

TITANIC

Perhaps it is inevitable that many myths have sprung up surrounding such a famous ship as *Titanic*. There is no shortage of material – from articles, books and documentaries – surrounding the ship's history and the disaster itself. However, their accuracy varies considerably, and when inaccurate or misleading information appears in one publication then it is apt to be cited in another; the process then continues. No one is perfect, even when every effort has been made to be accurate. It is also important to adopt a critical perspective, particularly with regard to conspiracy theories, or new interpretations of the disaster that are not rooted in a sound historical method or objective interpretation of *all* the evidence available.

Why did *Titanic* sink? The simple answer is that the damage sustained during the collision with the iceberg led to flooding that overwhelmed her watertight subdivision. It was also far beyond the capacity of the ship's pumps. The process has been illustrated simply by likening it to an ice-cube tray filling: one compartment is filled with water and then overflows into another. In reality, as the ship's bow settled lower in the water, the flooding progressed, permeating decks, stairways, ventilation and other openings; progressing gradually aft and exposing other openings as the bow submerged.

The fact that a number of the watertight bulkheads extended only to the underside of E-deck, or that there were no watertight decks 'sealing' each compartment, is sometimes cited as an example of inadequate design. However, the lack of a watertight deck was not an omission by Harland & Wolff but a design choice. There were real concerns that it might be dangerous in some circumstances, leading to a loss of stability or even a capsize if other damage resulted in flooding above the deck while air pockets remained beneath. Similarly, the bulkheads were high enough to keep the ship afloat with considerable flooding. She actually met a three-compartment standard under many scenarios; and even with the first four compartments flooded she would have remained afloat. None of this is to say that the design could not have been improved further, but it was not inherently faulty. Any ship will sink if it takes on too much water and *Titanic's* watertight subdivision meets *modern* standards. Passenger liners in the 1920s and 1930s would have fared no better with damage along the equivalent length.

Over two decades of exploring *Titanic's* wreck have shed light on the disaster and provided new information. In 1912, the resulting American and British investigations saw a number of witnesses testify. A strong majority did not say whether she sank intact or not; fourteen said she had broken apart and four said she had foundered intact.[3] The discovery of the wreck confirmed

that she did break up. Did that mean the ship was not strong enough? The answer is no. *Titanic's* hull failed when she was already in the final stages of sinking, after experiencing increasing stresses that reached about two and a half times the maximum that would be experienced in the most hostile North Atlantic storm.

Naval architecture is a progressive field. Ships grew larger and shipbuilders gained knowledge as they supplemented theory with practical experience. This

On 12 March 1914, A. Frederick Collins wrote an article asking 'Can the Lost *Titanic* be Raised?' It was accompanied by a diagram explaining: 'A western engineer's curious salvage scheme. He plans the raising of the ill-fated *Titanic* from the bottom of the sea, two miles below the surface, by means of many powerful magnets let down from a fleet of vessels. A submarine boat of special construction is an important factor in the project.' (*Leslie's Weekly*, 1914/Author's collection)

practical experience benefited each successive vessel and the next generation of liners. Generally speaking, they had a very good idea of the strength required and the stresses each vessel would bear. In comparing the 'Olympic' class ships with contemporaries such as Cunard's *Aquitania* and HAPAG's *Imperator*, which were built to the highest classification society standards by different builders, the similarities in their overall structures are remarkable. Experience from operating them yielded specific design improvements for future ships, particularly as they reached twenty years old, but Edward Wilding said that Harland & Wolff had needed to carry out fewer 'repairs to the *Olympic* than to any large ship we have ever built'. One qualified observer thought she had 'proved to be a successful ship in the matter of strength' in the 1920s.

It is sometimes said that *Titanic*'s expansion joints caused the ship to break apart. This, too, is false. Perhaps the argument is technical, but it is important. The hull itself gave *Titanic* her structural strength. The top of the hull was formed by B-deck. All the deckhouses on B, A and the boat decks, housing first-class staterooms, public rooms, the officers' quarters and the bridge, formed the superstructure. It sat *supra*, on top of the structural hull, almost as if the deckhouses were enclosures on a raft. They were comparatively lightly constructed and, because they were not designed to cope with the high stresses that the hull beneath endured, two expansion joints – essentially 'cuts' in the structure – divided the superstructure into three main sections. They allowed it to flex, as the hull beneath did in a seaway. They were not a perfect solution, but in general they did their job on *Olympic* for a quarter of a century, and *Britannic*'s design was refined further, based on experience with *Olympic* up to March 1912.

The expansion joints cannot be isolated entirely from the hull beneath, but the stresses borne by the vessel would be acting on the hull and *not* the superstructure. Once the hull was stressed to the point of failing, that failure had to begin somewhere. The areas in close proximity to expansion joints would be more likely to experience the initial failure, regardless of whether the ship broke initially from the top down or the bottom up, or from port or starboard. It does *not* follow that the failure began there. The hull would have failed if the superstructure and expansion joints had not existed.

Claims vary from simplistic to inaccurate. Was *Titanic*'s steel 'faulty'? It was tested to Lloyd's standards even though she was not built under the classification society's supervision. Certainly technology has advanced since she was built, but modern tests indicate 'it had sufficient fracture toughness, well within typical *modern* [original emphasis] fracture toughness values,

even at ice brine temperatures…'[4] What about the rivets? *Titanic* was built long before ships were entirely welded. A small number of rivets have been subjected to a recent study, including one hull rivet. While the iron rivets had an excessive quantity of slag, a residue from smelting that could make them more prone to fracture under stress, one iron rivet averaged only 1.1 per cent slag, substantially better than the required standards, but another measured 12.8 per cent. *Titanic*'s rivets did 'not represent an anomaly of the era' and 'at least some of the rivets would have failed no matter what their quality or strength'.[5] The collision appears to have stressed rivets in precisely the manner that would expose any weakness. It is hard to get away from the fact that a moving object weighing about 50,000 tons at the time of the collision and approaching at around 22.5 knots has enormous momentum. *Something* had to give way!

Sometimes myths and legends are more interesting than reality, but the reality is fascinating enough. There is no shortage of interest in the 'Olympic' class liners and the tragic fate that befell two of them, even 100 years later.

Notes

1   George Papatheodorou's article, 'Ghostly Images of HMHS *Britannic*', *Hydro International*, 2008. The survey was part of a habitat mapping project covering the Cyclades Islands (from the southern Aegean Sea to the eastern Mediterranean Sea), which was a collaborative effort between the Laboratory of Marine Geology and Physical Oceanography (MGPOL) and the Marine Biology Research Group of the Department of Geology and Biology of the University of Patras.

2   Carl Spencer's remarks are quoted from the answers to questions posed to him by *Britannic* researcher Michail Michailakis, with input from Remco Hillen and myself.

3   I am grateful to Bill Wormstedt for sharing his research and his article 'The Facts – What Did the Survivors See of the Break-up of the *Titanic*?' He maintains a website at: http://wormstedt.com/titanic

4   McCarty, Jennifer Hooper, and Foecke, Tim, *What Really Sank the Titanic* (Citadel Press: 2008), p.136.

5   McCarty, Jennifer Hooper, and Foecke, Tim, *Op. cit*, pp.144–47, 159, 164–66 and 170.

Appendix I

'OLYMPIC' CLASS SPECIFICATIONS

Celtic was the largest vessel in the world in 1901, but ten years later, *Olympic* was two and a half times larger measured by gross tonnage. Facts and figures help to demonstrate the '*Olympic*' class ships' size and capacities. Although designed for comfort rather than speed, to propel them at an average speed of 21 knots (over 24 land miles per hour) while retaining plenty of power in reserve required enormous propelling machinery.

	Olympic	Titanic	Britannic
Length overall	882ft 9in	882ft 9in	882ft 9in
Length between perpendiculars	850ft	850ft	850ft
Breadth, moulded	92ft	92ft	93ft 6in
Breadth, extreme	92ft 6in	92ft 6in	94ft
Gross Tonnage	45,323.82	46,328.59	48,157.90
Net Tonnage	20,894.20	21,831.34	24,592.24
Length, between perpendiculars	850ft	850ft	850ft
Breadth, moulded	92ft	92ft	93ft 6in
Depth, moulded	64ft 6in	64ft 6in	64ft 6in
Displacement	52,310	52,310	53,170
Registered displacement	77,780	77,780	78,950
Nominal horsepower	6,906	6,906	7,150
Indicated horsepower	50,000	50,000	50,000
Boilers	24 double ended, 5 single ended	24 double ended, 5 single ended	24 double ended (enlarged), 5 single ended
Pressure	215 pounds per square inch	215 pounds per square inch	215 pounds per square inch
Speed	21 knots	21 knots	21½ knots
First-class passengers	735	787	790
Second-class passengers	675	676	836
Third-class passengers	1,030	1,008	953

Appendix II

CONSTRUCTION CHRONOLOGY

Harland & Wolff's yard numbers 400, 401 and 433 were, successively, the largest vessels built by the company. *Olympic*'s construction took two and a half years from the laying of her keel to when she was delivered to the White Star Line. It is remarkable that the shipbuilder completed her so quickly, all while they worked on her sister ship. The progress of construction is apparent by examining these key dates:

	Olympic	Titanic	Britannic
Yard Number	400	401	433
Contracted for	31 July 1908	31 July 1908	23 October 1911
Order to proceed	17 September 1908 shipyard and engine works ordered to proceed 'except with [propelling] machinery'; 26 February 1909 shipyard and engine works ordered to proceed 'with boilers'; 20 April 1909 shipyard and engine works ordered to proceed 'with remainder of machinery'		28 June 1911 shipyard and engine works ordered to proceed
Keel laid	16 December 1908	31 March 1909	30 November 1911
Framed to height of the double bottom	10 March 1909	15 May 1909	12 March 1912
Fully framed	20 November 1909	6 April 1910	27 February 1913
Fully plated	15 April 1910	19 October 1910	20 September 1913
Launched	20 October 1910	31 May 1911	26 February 1914
Delivered	31 May 1911	2 April 1912	8 December 1915

Appendix III

COST OF THE 'OLYMPIC' CLASS

It is interesting to compare the cost of the 'Olympic' class ships with that of other vessels, to gain a better perspective of the expenses incurred by the White Star Line. *Celtic* and *Adriatic* were not built for the express service, nor was the smaller *Megantic*. Their costs were much lower. The figures illustrate how expensive the larger express ships were to construct. (There are many ways to compare money then and now. On a simple adjustment for retail price inflation, *Olympic*'s cost of £1,764,659 would be about £133,000,000 today.)

Celtic (1901)	Adriatic (1907)	Megantic (1909)	Olympic (1911)	Titanic (1912)	Britannic (1915)
£556,442	£632,464	£377,599	£1,764,659	£1,564,606	£1,947,797

Note: The final costs for all these vessels were taken from a listing of the White Star Line's fleet, showing their original costs and then the present values as at the end of 1916. They are cash figures, unadjusted for inflation. However, the figure for *Titanic* was unearthed by Mark Warren's research and *Britannic*'s was given following her loss. It should be noted that the figure for *Olympic* appears to include the costs of the 1913 refit.

Right: In July 1914, the Oceanic Steam Navigation Company made available their prospectus for a second issue of bonds, raising £1,500,000. Following J. Bruce Ismay's retirement the previous year, the company's chairman, Harold Sanderson, and fellow directors Lord Pirrie and E.C. Grenfell, signed off the document. The bonds were in denominations of £100 each. Applicants were instructed to send their payment to the company's bankers, Glyn, Mills, Currie & Co. of 67 Lombard Street, London, or the Bank of Liverpool, Liverpool. (National Archives, United Kingdom)

This Prospectus has been filed with the Registrar of Joint Stock Companies, in accordance with the Companies (Consolidation) Act, 1908.

The Subscription List will be closed on or before *Friday* the 10th July, 1914.

THE OCEANIC STEAM NAVIGATION COMPANY, LIMITED.

(*Incorporated under the Companies Act, 1862.*)

WHITE STAR LINE.

AUTHORISED ISSUE OF £3,375,000 4½ PER CENT. FIRST MORTGAGE DEBENTURES Divided into Debentures of the First and Second Series.

Trustees for the First Mortgage Debenture Holders:
THE HONOURABLE ALGERNON H. MILLS, 67, Lombard Street, London, E.C.
F. C. DANSON, Esq., Tower Buildings, Water Street, Liverpool.

Of the above Authorised Issue, the Debentures issued by the Company in 1908, of which there are £1,121,600 now outstanding, form the Debentures of the First Series, and £125,000 will be applied in redeeming these Debentures in each year ending 31st December up to 1921, by purchase at or under, or by drawings at, par. The balance of the Debentures of the First Series will be redeemed on the 30th June, 1922, at par. The Company is prohibited from issuing any further Debentures of the First Series.

The Debentures of the Second Series are limited to an amount which shall not at any time, together with the amount of the Debentures of the First Series for the time being outstanding, exceed £3,375,000 or 50 per cent. of the value of the assets specifically mortgaged whichever is less. During the year ending the 30th June, 1923, and during each succeeding year up to 1942, an amount equal to the greater of the following sums : (1) £125,000, or (2) a sum equal to 5 per cent. on the amount of the Debentures of the Second Series outstanding at the commencement of such year, will be applied in the redemption of debentures of the Second Series by purchase at or under, or by drawings at, par. The balance of the Debentures of the Second Series will be redeemed on the 30th June, 1943, at par. After the 30th June, 1923, the Company is prohibited from issuing any Debentures of the Second Series to replace the Debentures to be so redeemed.

Interest payable 30th June and 31st December.

Messrs. GLYN, MILLS, CURRIE & CO., 67, Lombard Street, London, as Bankers of the Company, are authorised to receive subscriptions for:

£1,500,000 4½ per Cent. FIRST MORTGAGE DEBENTURES

SECOND SERIES.

ISSUE PRICE £95 per Cent. payable as follows:—

£ 5 per Cent. on Application.	
£30 " on Allotment,	
£30 " on 30th September, 1914,	
£30 " on 30th November, 1914.	
£95 per Cent.	

Payment may be made in full on allotment or on either of the subsequent instalment dates, under discount at the rate of £3 per cent. per annum.

The whole Issue of £3,375,000 First Mortgage Debentures will be secured by a specific First Mortgage upon 24 steamships of the Company and upon a new steamship, the "Britannic," now building, which vessel is to be in commission early in 1915, and by a floating charge on all other the assets of the Company. The gross tonnage of these 25 vessels exceeds 419,000 tons, and their present value at cost, less depreciation at the rate of 5 per cent. per annum to 31st December, 1913, exceeds £6,500,000.

The net earnings of the Company after charging all outgoings, including repairs and renewals and all expenses of management, but before charging interest and providing for depreciation, have been certified for the past 10 years by Messrs. Price, Waterhouse & Co., the Company's Auditors, as under :—

Year		Year	
1904	£502,730	1909	£613,054
1905	712,679	1910	1,057,519
1906	805,309	1911	1,073,752
1907	848,486	1912	885,332
1908	298,941	1913	1,080,918

Average of 10 years £787,872.

The average net earnings therefore cover more than six times the interest on both the Debentures now offered for subscription and the outstanding Debentures.

The Debentures of the Second Series rank *pari passu* in point of charge with the Debentures of the First Series.

BIBLIOGRAPHY AND ACKNOWLEDGEMENTS

SECONDARY SOURCES AND PUBLISHED WORKS

Bäbler, Günter. 'The Dinner at Lord Pirrie's in Summer 1907: Just a Legend?' *Titanic Post,* June 2000, vol.32.

Beaumont, John C.H., *Ships and People* (Geoffrey Bles: 1926).

Bemis, Albert Farwell, *A Journey to India* (Private Printing: 1923).

Brome, Vincent, *J.B. Priestley* (Hamish Hamilton Ltd: 1988).

Beveridge, Bruce, Scott Andrews, Steve Hall, Daniel Klistorner and Art Braunschweiger (eds) *Titanic: The Ship Magnificent.* (The History Press: 2008).

Bullock, Shan F., *Thomas Andrews: Shipbuilder* (Maunsel & Company Ltd:1912).

Chirnside, Mark, 'Target *Olympic: Feure!*', *Titanic Commutator,* 2008, vol.32, no.184.

——, *The 'Olympic' Class Ships: Olympic Titanic Britannic* (The History Press: 2011).

——, *RMS Aquitania: The 'Ship Beautiful'* (The History Press: 2008).

——, '*Lusitania* and *Mauretania*: Perceptions of Popularity', *Titanic Commutator,* 2008, vol.32, no.184.

——, *RMS Majestic: The 'Magic Stick'* (Tempus Publishing: 2006).

——, *RMS Olympic: Titanic's Sister* (Tempus Publishing: 2004).

——, and Sam Halpern, '*Olympic* and *Titanic*: Maiden Voyage Mysteries', *Voyage,* 2007.

——, and Paul Lee, 'The *Gigantic* Question', *Titanic Commutator,* 2008, vol.31 no.180.

Cooke, Anthony, '*Olympic* and *Titanic*: How Many Masts?', *Sea Lines,* 2006, issue 42.

Garzke, William H., & John Woodward, *Titanic Ships: Titanic Disasters: An Analysis of Early White Star and Cunard Superliners* (The Society of Naval Architects and Marine Engineers: 2002).

Gilpin, Sandra, '"Always Faithful": Thomas Andrews and the *Titanic*', *The Non-Subscribing Presbyterian,* April 2002, no.1145.

Hayes, Captain Bertram Fox, *Hull Down* (Cassell & Co.: 1925).

Kirk, Richard, 'Part Four: The Final Journey of the *Britannic…*', *Titanic Commutator,* 1991, vol.15.

Lawrence, A.H., *Duke Ellington and His World* (Routledge: 2003).

McCarty, Jennifer Hooper and Tim Foecke, *What Really Sank the Titanic* (Citadel Press: 2008).

Mills, Simon, *Hostage to Fortune,* (Wordsmith Publications: 2002).

Oldham, Wilton J., *The Ismay Line,* (The Journal of Commerce: 1961).

Papatheodorou, George, 'Ghostly Images of HMHS *Britannic*', *Hydro International,* 2008.

Parker, Captain Walter H., *Leaves from an Unwritten Log Book* (Sampson Low, Marston & Co. Ltd: 1931).

Strouse, Jean, *Morgan: American Financier* (Perennial: 2000).

Weaver, Maurice and Edwin Steel, with Brian Ticehurst, '*Titanic's* Sister Ship Headed for the Rocks', *Titanic Commutator,* 1988, vol.XII.

ARCHIVAL SOURCES

National Archives (The Public Records Office)
ADM 53/21870; ADM 137/1012; ADM 186/38; BT 100/245-484; MT 9/920/E; MT 9/1146; MT 10/1424; MT 10/1805; MT 15/150; MT 15/229; MT 15/465; MT 15/504; MT 15/530; MT 15/680; MT 15/692; MT 23/420; MT 23/501; MT 23/535; MT 23/593; MT 23/601; MT 23/615-16; MT 23/637; MT 23/638; MT 23/781; TS 36/175-76, 183-85, 195.

National Archives of Canada
Militia and Defence Canadian Expeditionary Force, 1914–19; War Diaries, First World War, 1914–19. RG 9, III, D 3, vol.5056, July 1916.

National Museums Liverpool (Maritime Archives & Library, Merseyside Maritime Museum)
B/CUN/3/17/1; B/CUN/4/4/5; DX 504/7/1; DX/504/8-10; DX/504/12/4.

The Cunard Archive, Sydney Jones Library, Liverpool University
D42 – AC14/35; ASC12/4A-B; ASC12/10; B2; B4/44; B5/1-2; GM3/1-2; GM4;
GM11; GM13/6; GM14A-B; S/37/3/75; S10/5.

The Imperial War Museum, London
The Papers of Private Robert Edward Atkinson, 95/1/1; The Papers of Miss E.
Barber, 99/76/1; The Papers of Miss Ada Garland, 77/57/1; The Papers of Miss W.
Greenwood, 87/33/1; The Papers of Corporal Frank Leslie Stone, 02/55/1.

**United States National Archives and Records Administration,
Washington**
Olympic, Box 55; Office of Naval Intelligence Reports on Camouflaged Ships
1918, Entry 156; Records of the Office of the Chief of Naval Operations, Record
Group 38; National Archives Building, Washington, DC.

★

First and foremost, my deep and enduring gratitude to my parents, family and friends
who offered so much support and encouragement. Thanks are due to so many kind
people for being generous with their time: helping to answer questions, finding
material to share and offering warm words and encouragement. In a number of cases,
their assistance was not for a specific project, but serves as an ongoing contribution: for
example, in helping to identify a particular photograph that has been used; or sharing
material that assisted my research in the past and continues to colour my perspective:

Steve Anderson; Scott Andrews; Günter Bäbler; Catherine R. Bernstein;
Bruce Beveridge; Leigh Bishop; Joe Carvalho; John Chatterton; Cyril Codus;
Lionel Codus; Richard de Kerbrech; Shelley Dzeidzic; John Eaton; Franck
Gavard-Parret; Sandra Gilpin; Dave Gittins; Jarrod Jablonski; Charles Haas; Steve
Hall; Sam Halpern; Brian Hawley; Mrs C. R. Hayton; Rebecca Hoad; Brent
Holt; Nick Hope; David Hutchings; Jennifer Irwin; Ed and Karen Kamuda; Stuart
Kelly; Arnold Kludas; Richie Kohler; J. Kent Layton; Oliver Loerscher; Gerry
Livadas; Eric Longo; Michael Lowrey; Ken Marschall; John Maxtone-Graham;
Ken McLeod; Ryan McMillen; Roy Mengot; Michail Michailakis; Simon Mills;
Norman Morse; Susan Osborne Jones; Mike Poirier; Bob Read; Mary Anne
Sharpe; Inger Sheil; Jonathan Smith; Tarn Stephanos; Parks Stephenson; Richard
Stevenson; Hilary Thomas; Mark Warren; Stuart Williamson; Bill Wormstedt.
Stuart Williamson painted the wonderful image of *Britannic*'s final moments
and kindly consented to its reproduction. He maintains a website at: http://
website.lineone.net/~stu_williamson and invites commissions. Cyril Codus, who
depicted *Britannic* as a hospital ship, is online at: http://www.tianic.skyrock.com
[sic]; Lionel Codus, who redrew the 'Design "D"' *Olympic-Titanic* concept from
July 1908, is at: http://adesdubd.skyrock.com.
    A particular vote of thanks is due to a number of individuals who have gone
out of their way to assist, even while there were many demands on their own
time, whether by sharing their own research and illustrations or answering
my numerous questions. They include Scott Andrews, Günter Bäbler, Bruce
Beveridge, Ralph Currell, Ioannis Georgiou and Daniel Klistorner.
    Organisations and individuals have been extremely helpful. It would not
be possible to write a history of this sort without the remarkable (and often
monotonous) work that archivists, conservationists, museum staff and others do
to restore, preserve, catalogue and make available historical records. Steve van
Dulken, Lisa Kenny and the staff of the British Library; Robert Gallagher and
the staff of British Pathé; The Canadian Letters and Images Project, Department
of History at Malaspina University College; the staff of special collections, the
Cunard Archives at Liverpool University's Sydney Jones Library; Charlotte Kidd
and the staff of Classic Lodges, the White Swan Hotel; Jane Humphrey, Diane
Matthews and the staff of Dudley Archives and Local History Service; Alison
Heald and the staff of the curator's department at Hampton Court Palace; Simon
Offord, Anthony Richards and the staff of the Imperial War Museum; Alison
Cullingford, J.B. Priestley Archive, Special Collections, University of Bradford, and
the PFD agency, acting on behalf of the estate of J.B. Priestley. David Rumsey and
Christoph Haenggi, Museum für Musikautomaten, Seewen, Switzerland; the staff
of the Public Records Office of Northern Ireland (PRONI), with thanks given
to the Deputy Keeper of the Records at the Public Records Office of Northern
Ireland and Harland & Wolff; the staff of the Scout Information Centre; Michelle
Ashmore, Michael McCaughan, George Wright and the staff of the Ulster Folk
& Transport Museum, National Museums Northern Ireland; Mary Ann Bader,
United States Coast Guard, and Bob Mannino, United States Lightship Museum;
Charles Mazoujian for kindly allowing me to use his wonderful painting, and his
daughter Gwen Mazoujian for her assistance; Gregory Plunges and the staff of the
United States National Archives and Records Administration. There are several
other organisations who helped by supplying images, and they are acknowledged
specifically alongside the relevant illustration.
    The book's format is not that of a heavy academic tome; however it is hoped that
the select list of some of the primary sources consulted will be a useful reference for
someone interested in a particular aspect of the subject. I am most grateful to Sue
Garland, the copyright holder of the papers of Miss Ada Garland, and Mrs Grace
Wallis, the copyright holder of the papers of Private Robert Edward Atkinson.
Wherever possible, I have sought to locate the relevant copyright holders, however
in a number of instances this has not been possible. I would therefore like to extend
my thanks to those who have made available publicly – through museum donations
and other means – documents that help us to gain a better understanding of the
events of the past. I also offer my sincere apologies to anyone who I may have
inadvertently failed to acknowledge. If any mistakes like that have arisen then I will
be more than happy to correct them in any future editions; and in the meantime I
can only offer my heartfelt regret and apologies.
    Finally, my sincere thanks and gratitude to my editor Amy Rigg and her team
of Emily Locke, Siubhan Macdonald and Marc Williams, and everyone at The
History Press for finally making this book a reality.

THE TITANIC COLLECTION

THE 100TH ANNIVERSARY OF THE SINKING OF TITANIC 15TH APRIL 2012

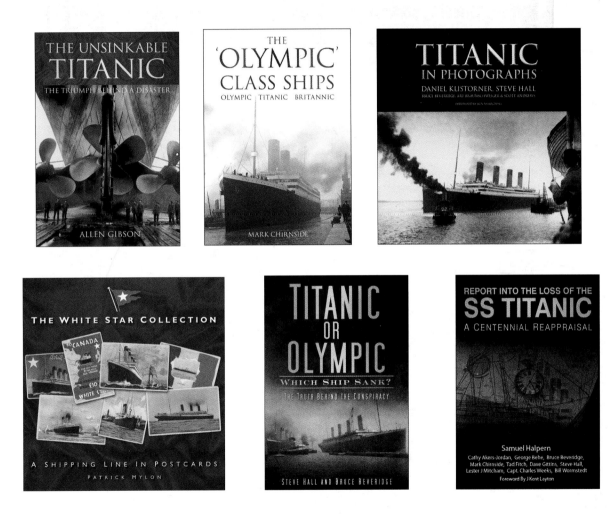

THE UNSINKABLE TITANIC
THE TRIUMPH BEHIND A DISASTER
ALLEN GIBSON

THE 'OLYMPIC' CLASS SHIPS
OLYMPIC TITANIC BRITANNIC
MARK CHIRNSIDE

TITANIC IN PHOTOGRAPHS
DANIEL KLISTORNER, STEVE HALL
BRUCE BEVERIDGE, ART BRAUNSCHWEIGER & SCOTT ANDREWS
FOREWORD BY KEN MARSCHALL

THE WHITE STAR COLLECTION
A SHIPPING LINE IN POSTCARDS
PATRICK MYLON

TITANIC OR OLYMPIC
WHICH SHIP SANK?
THE TRUTH BEHIND THE CONSPIRACY
STEVE HALL AND BRUCE BEVERIDGE

REPORT INTO THE LOSS OF THE SS TITANIC
A CENTENNIAL REAPPRAISAL
Samuel Halpern
Cathy Akers-Jordan, George Behe, Bruce Beveridge,
Mark Chirnside, Tad Fitch, Dave Gittins, Steve Hall,
Lester J Mitcham, Capt. Charles Weeks, Bill Wormstedt
Foreword By J Kent Layton

For the full Titanic experience visit The History Press website and follow the Titanic link

www.thehistorypress.co.uk

For stories and articles about Titanic, join us on Facebook

The History Press